Weather and Climate Inventory National Park Service Northeast Temperate Network

Natural Resource Technical Report NPS/NETN/NRTR—2006/011
WRCC Report 2006-10

Christopher A. Davey, Kelly T. Redmond, and David B. Simeral
Western Regional Climate Center
Desert Research Institute
2215 Raggio Parkway
Reno, Nevada 89512-1095

November 2006

U.S. Department of the Interior
National Park Service
Natural Resource Program Center
Fort Collins, Colorado

The Natural Resource Publication series addresses natural resource topics that are of interest and applicability to a broad readership in the National Park Service and to others in the management of natural resources, including the scientific community, the public, and the National Park Service conservation and environmental constituencies. Manuscripts are peer-reviewed to ensure that the information is scientifically credible, technically accurate, appropriately written for the intended audience, and designed and published in a professional manner.

The Natural Resources Technical Reports series is used to disseminate the peer-reviewed results of scientific studies in the physical, biological, and social sciences for both the advancement of science and the achievement of the National Park Service mission. The reports provide contributors with a forum for displaying comprehensive data that are often deleted from journals because of page limitations. Current examples of such reports include the results of research that address natural resource management issues; natural resource inventory and monitoring activities; resource assessment reports; scientific literature reviews; and peer-reviewed proceedings of technical workshops, conferences, or symposia.

Views and conclusions in this report are those of the authors and do not necessarily reflect policies of the National Park Service. Mention of trade names or commercial products does not constitute endorsement or recommendation for use by the National Park Service.

Printed copies of reports in these series may be produced in a limited quantity and they are only available as long as the supply lasts. This report is also available from the Natural Resource Publications Management website (http://www.nature.nps.gov/publications/NRPM) on the Internet or by sending a request to the address on the back cover.

Please cite this publication as follows:

Davey, C. A., K. T. Redmond, and D. B. Simeral. 2006. Weather and Climate Inventory, National Park Service, Northeast Temperate Network. Natural Resource Technical Report NPS/NETN/NRTR—2006/011. National Park Service, Fort Collins, Colorado.

NPS/NETN/NRTR—2006/011, November 2006

Contents

Contents (continued)

Figures

Tables

Appendixes

Acronyms

AASC	American Association of State Climatologists
ACAD	Acadia National Park
ACIS	Applied Climate Information System
APPA	Appalachian National Scenic Trail
ASOS	Automated Surface Observing System
AWOS	Automated Weather Observing System
BLM	Bureau of Land Management
BOHA	Boston Harbor Islands National Recreation Area
CASTNet	Clean Air Status and Trends Network
COOP	Cooperative Observer Program
CWOP	Citizen Weather Observer Program
DFIR	Double-Fence Intercomparison Reference
DST	daylight savings time
EPA	Environmental Protection Agency
FAA	Federal Aviation Administration
FIPS	Federal Information Processing Standards
GMT	Greenwich Mean Time
GOES	Geostationary Operational Environmental Satellite
GPMP	Gaseous Pollutant Monitoring Program
GPS	Global Positioning System
GPS-MET	NOAA ground-based GPS meteorology
GRSM	Great Smoky Mountains National Park
I&M	NPS Inventory and Monitoring Program
LST	local standard time
MABI	Marsh-Billings-Rockefeller National Historical Park
MIMA	Minute Man National Historical Park
MORR	Morristown National Historical Park
NADP	National Atmospheric Deposition Program
NAO-AO	North Atlantic Oscillation – Arctic Oscillation
NCDC	National Climatic Data Center
NetCDF	Network Common Data Form
NERCC	Northeast Regional Climate Center
NETN	Northeast Temperate Inventory and Monitoring Network
NOAA	National Oceanic and Atmospheric Administration
NPS	National Park Service
NRCS	Natural Resources Conservation Service
NWS	National Weather Service
POMS	Portable Ozone Monitoring System
PRISM	Parameter Regression on Independent Slopes Model
RAWS	Remote Automated Weather Station Network
RCC	regional climate center
ROVA	Roosevelt – Vanderbilt National Historic Site
SAGA	Saint-Gaudens National Historic Site

SAIR	Saugus Iron Works National Historic Site
SAO	Surface Airways Observation Network
SARA	Saratoga National Historical Park
SCAN	Soil Climate Analysis Network
SHEN	Shenandoah National Park
SOD	Summary Of the Day
Surfrad	Surface Radiation Budget Network
SNOTEL	Snowfall Telemetry Network
USDA	U.S. Department of Agriculture
USGS	U.S. Geological Survey
UTC	Coordinated Universal Time
WBAN	Weather Bureau Army Navy
WEFA	Weir Farm National Historic Site
WMO	World Meteorological Organization
WRCC	Western Regional Climate Center
WX4U	Weather For You network

Executive Summary

Climate is a dominant factor driving the physical and ecologic processes affecting the Northeast Temperate Inventory and Monitoring Network (NETN). Climate variations are responsible for short- and long-term changes in ecosystem fluxes of energy and matter and have profound effects on underlying geomorphic and biogeochemical processes. The temperate deciduous forest biome, common to the NETN, is one of the biomes most impacted worldwide by human stresses. These stresses influence directly the local and regional climate characteristics in the NETN and contribute significantly to climate changes in the area. Extreme storm events such as ice storms, nor'easters, and tropical systems are known to impact NETN ecosystems. The ice storm of January 1998 was one of the most damaging ice storms on record, significantly disturbing the temperate forests of the NETN. Because of its influence on the ecology of NETN park units and the surrounding areas, climate was identified as a high-priority, vital sign for NETN, and climate is one of the 12 basic inventories to be completed for all National Park Service (NPS) Inventory and Monitoring Program (I&M) networks.

This project was initiated to inventory past and present climate monitoring efforts in the NETN. In this report, we provide the following information:

- Overview of broad-scale climatic factors and zones important to NETN park units.
- Inventory of weather and climate station locations in and near NETN park units relevant to the NPS I&M Program.
- Results of an inventory of metadata on each weather station, including affiliations for weather-monitoring networks, types of measurements recorded at these stations, and information about the actual measurements (length of record, etc.).
- Initial evaluation of the adequacy of coverage for existing weather stations and recommendations for improvements in monitoring weather and climate.

In addition, we also provide an overview of weather and climate monitoring efforts for the Appalachian National Scenic Trail (APPA). Numerous stations, both manual and automated, are available for weather- and climate-monitoring efforts along APPA. Several key stations are located along or very near the trail, including Clingmans Dome in Great Smoky Mountains National Park (GRSM) in North Carolina, Big Meadows in Shenandoah National Park (SHEN) in Virginia, and the summit of Mt. Washington in New Hampshire.

Topography and proximity to the Atlantic Ocean both influence the overall climate characteristics of the NETN. North-south gradients are present in the NETN for precipitation and temperature. Mean annual temperatures in the NETN range from around 5°C at MABI to 9°C at Morristown National Historical Park (MORR) and Weir Farm National Historic Site (WEFA). Temperatures vary greatly throughout the year in the NETN. Cold-air outbreaks have dropped air temperatures to as low as -40°C for interior park units, while summertime temperatures have reached 40°C in southern portions of the NETN. The driest park units in the NETN, Saint-Gaudens National Historic Site (SAGA) and Saratoga National Historical Park (SARA), are located in lower-elevation interior areas, with mean annual precipitation totals below 1000 mm. Park units closer to the Atlantic, such as Acadia National Park (ACAD), MORR, and WEFA, are wetter with mean annual precipitation totals that approach 1400 mm. Much precipitation in the

NETN is associated with nor'easters, which are strong low-pressure centers that develop along the Atlantic Ocean's Gulf Stream current and move northeastward along the east coast of the U.S. Local topography provides orographic enhancement of the precipitation, especially in the higher elevations of the NETN. Convective processes contribute a small portion of the precipitation during the spring and summer months. Snowfall contributes significantly to yearly precipitation in interior portions of the NETN.

Although precipitation occurs regularly throughout the year in the NETN, winter precipitation is more common in the northern/eastern portions of the NETN while summer precipitation is more common in the southern/western portions of the NETN. The Northern Atlantic Oscillation – Arctic Oscillation influences interannual temperature variations in the NETN. Long-term trends in temperature and precipitation in the NETN are still not well defined.

Through a search of national databases and inquiries to NPS staff, we have identified five weather and climate stations within NETN park units. These include four stations in ACAD and one station in SARA. The National Weather Service (NWS) Cooperative Observer Program (COOP) station at ACAD is the only active COOP station within 30 km of ACAD that has a data record longer than two decades, making it essential that NPS actively work with the NWS forecast offices in this region to help ensure that this valuable station remains active for NPS research and management activities. The only source of automated weather data we identified inside ACAD is the Gaseous Pollutant Monitoring Program (GPMP) station on Cadillac Mountain. For weather conditions at sea level, ACAD must utilize observations from the Surface Airways Observation Network (SAO) stations at Bar Harbor Airport and the various light stations along the coast near ACAD. The SAO station at Bar Harbor Airport is also the best source for long-term climate records for ACAD.

Due to the small number of weather/climate stations within NETN park units, it is important for NETN park units to rely on outside sources of weather and climate data. Most of the NETN park units have a relatively dense coverage of nearby weather/climate stations. This is true especially for the park units near Boston and New York City. Most of these park units have several nearby COOP stations that have lengthy periods of record. Near-real-time observations are generally available from SAO station located at major airports, especially in the Boston and New York City regions. The one exception to this general pattern appears to be MORR, which despite its location within the suburbs west of New York City, has no active COOP stations and only one airport station within 10 km of the park unit. The best sources for near-real-time data may therefore be from the SAO stations at Teterboro Airport, Newark International Airport and the international airports in New York City. All of these are at least 30 km east of MORR.

Acknowledgements

This work was supported and completed under Task Agreement H8R07010001, with the Great Basin Cooperative Ecosystem Studies Unit. We would like to acknowledge very helpful assistance from various National Park Service personnel associated with the Northeast Temperate Inventory and Monitoring Network. Particular thanks are extended to Greg Shriver, Fred Dieffenbach, and Theresa Moore. We also thank John Gross, Margaret Beer, Grant Kelly, Greg McCurdy, and Heather Angeloff for all their help. Seth Gutman with the National Oceanic and Atmospheric Administration Earth Systems Research Laboratory provided valuable input on the GPS-MET station network. Portions of the work were supported by the NOAA Western Regional Climate Center.

1.0. Introduction

Weather and climate are key drivers in ecosystem structure, composition, and function. Global- and regional-scale climate variations will have a tremendous impact on natural systems (Chapin et al. 1996; Schlesinger 1997; Jacobson et al. 2000; Bonan 2002). Long-term patterns in temperature and precipitation provide first-order constraints on potential ecosystem structure and function. Secondary constraints are realized from the intensity and duration of individual weather events and, additionally, from seasonality and inter-annual climate variability. These constraints influence the fundamental properties of ecologic systems, such as soil–water relationships, plant–soil processes, and nutrient cycling, as well as disturbance rates and intensity. These properties, in turn, influence the life-history strategies supported by a climatic regime (Neilson 1987; Shriver et al. 2005).

Given the importance of climate, it is one of 12 basic inventories to be completed by the National Park Service (NPS) Inventory and Monitoring Program (I&M) network (I&M 2006). As primary environmental drivers for the other vital signs, weather and climate patterns present various practical and management consequences and implications for the NPS (Oakley et al. 2003). Most park units observe weather and climate elements as part of their overall mission. The lands under NPS stewardship provide many excellent locations for monitoring climatic conditions.

The purpose of this report is to determine the current status of weather and climate monitoring within the Northeast Temperate Inventory and Monitoring Network (NETN; Figure 1.1; Table 1.1). A brief summary of current weather and climate monitoring efforts along the Appalachian National Scenic Trail (APPA) is also included (Appendix A). In this report, we provide the following informational elements:

- Overview of broad-scale climatic factors and zones important to NETN park units.
- Inventory of locations for all weather stations in and near NETN park units that are relevant to the NPS I&M networks.
- Results of metadata inventory for each station, including weather-monitoring network affiliations, types of recorded measurements, and information about actual measurements (length of record, etc.).
- Initial evaluation of the adequacy of coverage for existing weather stations and recommendations for improvements in monitoring weather and climate.

It is essential that park units within the NETN have an effective climate-monitoring system in place to track climate changes and to aid in management decisions relating to these changes. The primary objectives for climate- and weather-monitoring in NETN are as follows (Shriver et al. 2005):

A. Determine long-term trends in average monthly maximum temperature, average monthly minimum temperature, average monthly mean temperature, and total monthly precipitation in NETN parks.
B. Correlate weather trends with trends observed in data collected with other protocols (e.g., phenology) to determine the extent to which weather trends can explain trends in monitoring data.

1

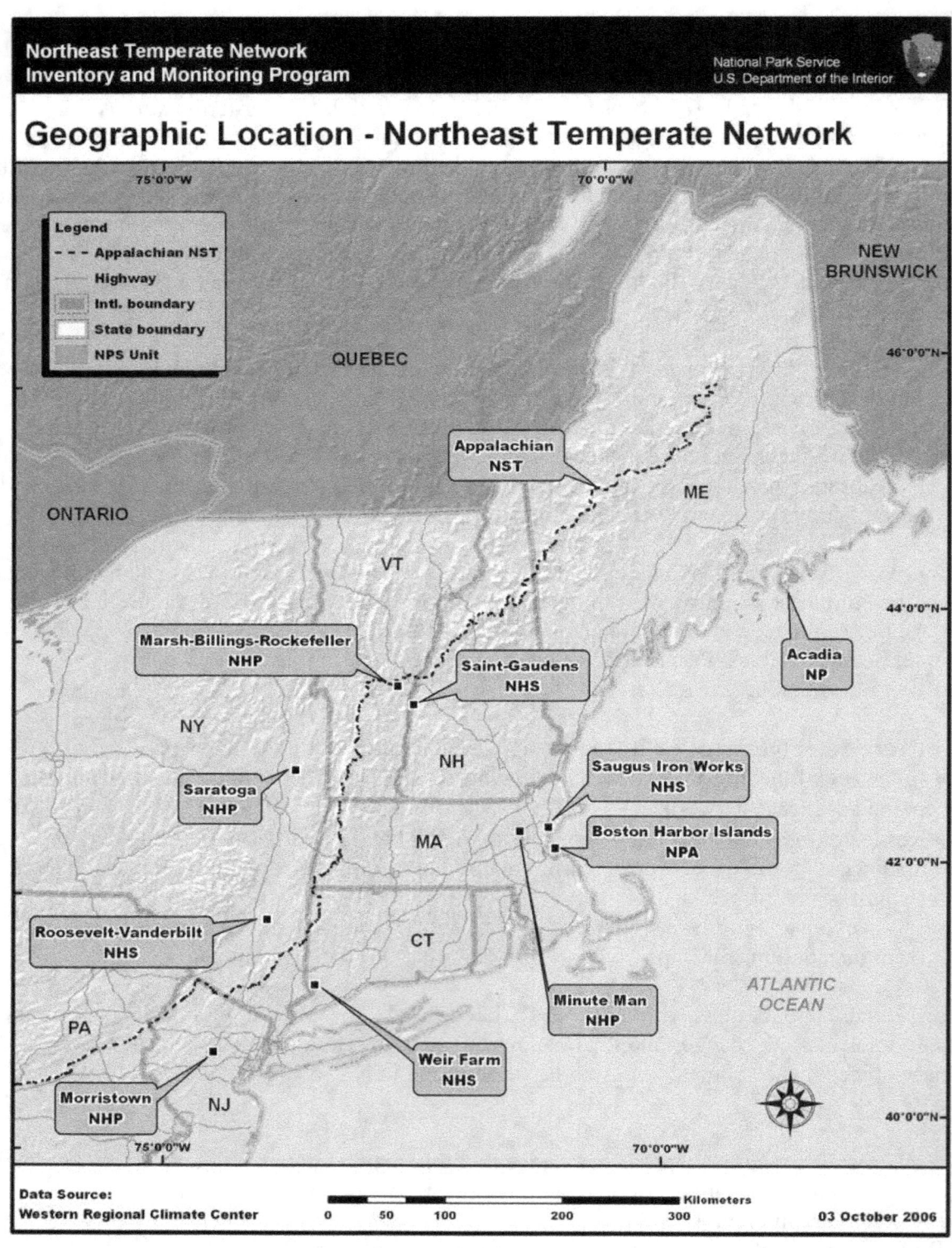

Figure 1.1. Map of the Northeast Temperate Network.

Table 1.1. Park units in the NETN.

Acronym	Name
ACAD	Acadia National Park
BOHA	Boston Harbor Islands National Recreation Area
MABI	Marsh-Billings-Rockefeller National Historical Park
MIMA	Minute Man National Historical Park
MORR	Morristown National Historical Park
ROVA	Roosevelt-Vanderbilt National Historic Site
SAGA	Saint-Gaudens National Historic Site
SAIR	Saugus Iron Works National Historic Site
SARA	Saratoga National Historical Park
WEFA	Weir Farm National Historic Site

1.1. Network Terminology

Before proceeding, it is important to stress that this report discusses the idea of "networks" in two different ways. Modifiers are used to distinguish between NPS I&M networks and weather/climate station networks. See Appendix B for a full definition of these terms.

1.1.1. Weather/Climate Station Networks

Most weather and climate measurements are made not from isolated stations but from stations that are part of a network operated in support of a particular mission. The limiting case is a network of one station, where measurements are made by an interested observer or group. Larger networks usually have more and better inventory data and station-tracking procedures. Some national weather/climate networks are associated with the National Oceanic and Atmospheric Administration (NOAA), including the National Weather Service (NWS) Cooperative Observer Program (COOP). Other national networks include the interagency Remote Automated Weather Station Network (RAWS) and the U.S. Department of Agriculture/Natural Resources Conservation Service (USDA/NRCS) Snowfall Telemetry (SNOTEL) and snowcourse networks. Usually a single agency, but sometimes a consortium of interested parties, will jointly support a particular weather/climate network.

1.1.2. NPS I&M Networks

Within the NPS, the system for monitoring various attributes in the participating park units (about 270–280 in total) is divided into 32 NPS I&M networks. These networks are collections of park units grouped together around a common theme, typically geographical.

1.2. Weather versus Climate Definitions

It is important to establish whether the primary use of a given station is for weather purposes or for climate purposes. Weather station networks are intended for near-real-time usage, where the precise circumstances of a set of measurements are typically less important. In these cases, changes in exposure or other attributes over time are not as critical. Climate networks, however, are intended for long-term tracking of atmospheric conditions. Siting and exposure are critical factors for climate networks, and it is vitally important that the observational circumstances remain essentially unchanged over the duration of the station record. Some climate networks can be considered hybrids of weather/climate networks. These hybrid climate networks can supply information on a short-term "weather" time scale and a longer-term "climate" time scale.

In this report, "weather" generally refers to current (or near-real-time) atmospheric conditions, while "climate" is defined as the complete ensemble of statistical descriptors for temporal and spatial properties of atmospheric behavior (see Appendix B). Climate and weather phenomena shade gradually into each other and are ultimately inseparable.

1.3. Purpose of Measurement

Climatologically-focused inventory and monitoring climate activities should be based on a set of fundamental guiding principles. Any evaluation of weather/climate monitoring programs begins with asking the following question:

- What is the purpose of weather and climate measurements?

Evaluation of past, present, or planned weather/climate monitoring activities must be based on the answer to this question.

Weather and climate data and information constitute a prominent and widely requested component of the NPS I&M networks (I&M 2006). Within the context of the NPS, the following services constitute the main purposes for recording weather and climate observations:

- Provide measurements for real-time operational needs and early warnings of potential hazards (landslides, mudflows, washouts, fallen trees, plowing activities, fire conditions, aircraft and watercraft conditions, road conditions, rescue conditions, fog, restoration and remediation activities, etc.).
- Provide visitor education and aid interpretation of expected and actual conditions for visitors while they are in the park and for deciding if and when to visit the park.
- Establish engineering and design criteria for structures, roads, culverts, etc., for human comfort, safety, and economic needs.
- Consistently monitor climate over the long-term to detect changes in environmental drivers affecting ecosystems, including both gradual and sudden events.
- Provide retrospective data to understand *a posteriori* changes in flora and fauna.
- Document for posterity the physical conditions in and near the park units, including mean, extreme, and variable measurements (in time and space) for all applications.

The last three items in the preceding list are pertinent primarily to the NPS I&M networks; however, all items are important to NPS operations and management. Most of the needs in this list overlap heavily. It is often impractical to operate separate climate measuring systems that also cannot be used to meet ordinary weather needs, where there is greater emphasis on timeliness and reliability.

1.4. Design of Climate-Monitoring Programs

Determining the purposes for collecting measurements in a given weather/climate monitoring program will guide the process of identifying weather/climate stations suitable for the monitoring program. The context for making these decisions is provided in Chapter 2 where background on the NETN climate is presented. However, this process is only one step in evaluating and designing a climate-monitoring program. This process includes the following additional steps:

- Define park and network-specific monitoring needs and objectives.
- Identify locations and data repositories of existing and historic stations.
- Acquire existing data when necessary or practical.
- Evaluate the quality of existing data.
- Evaluate the adequacy of coverage of existing stations.
- Develop a protocol for monitoring the weather and climate, including the following:
  o Standardized summaries and reports of weather/climate data.
  o Data management (quality assurance and quality control, archiving, data access, etc.).
- Develop and implement a plan for installing or modifying stations, as necessary.

Throughout the design process, there are various factors that require consideration in evaluating weather and climate measurements. Many of these factors have been summarized by Dr. Tom Karl, director of the NOAA National Climatic Data Center (NCDC), and widely distributed as the "Ten Principles for Climate Monitoring" (Karl et al. 1996a; NRC 2001). These principals are presented in Appendix C, and the guidelines are embodied in many of the comments made throughout this report. The most critical factors are presented here. In addition, an overview of requirements necessary to operate a climate network is provided in Appendix D, with further discussion in Appendix E.

1.4.1. Need for Consistency
A principal goal in climate monitoring is to detect and characterize slow and sudden changes in climate through time. This is of less concern for day-to-day weather changes, but it is of paramount importance for climate variability and change. There are many ways whereby changes in techniques for making measurements, changes in instruments or their exposures, or seemingly innocuous changes in site characteristics can lead to apparent changes in climate. Safeguards must be in place to avoid these false sources of temporal "climate" variability if we are to draw correct inferences about climate behavior over time from archived measurements.

For climate monitoring, consistency through time is vital, counting at least as important as absolute accuracy. Sensors record only what is occurring at the sensor—this is all they can detect. It is the responsibility of station or station network managers to ensure that observations are representative of the spatial and temporal climate scales that we wish to record.

1.4.2. Metadata
Changes in instruments, site characteristics, and observing methodologies can lead to apparent changes in climate through time. It is therefore vital to document all factors that can bear on the interpretation of climate measurements and to update the information repeatedly through time. This information ("metadata," data about data) has its own history and set of quality-control issues that parallel those of the actual data. There is no single standard for the content of climate metadata, but a simple rule suffices:

- Observers should record all information that could be needed in the future to interpret observations correctly without benefit of the observers' personal recollections.

Such documentation includes notes, drawings, site forms, and photos, which can be of inestimable value if taken in the correct manner. That stated, it is not always clear to the metadata provider *what is important* for posterity and *what will be important* in the future. It is almost impossible to "over document" a station. Station documentation is greatly underappreciated and is seldom thorough enough (especially for climate purposes). Insufficient attention to this issue often lowers the present and especially future value of otherwise useful data.

The convention followed throughout climatology is to refer to metadata as information about the measurement process, station circumstances, and data. The term "data" is reserved solely for the actual weather and climate records obtained from sensors.

1.4.3. Maintenance
Inattention to maintenance is the greatest source of failure in weather/climate stations and networks. Problems begin to occur soon after sites are deployed. A regular visit schedule must be implemented, where sites, settings (e.g., vegetation), sensors, communications, and data flow are checked routinely (once or twice a year at a minimum) and updated as necessary. Parts must be changed out for periodic recalibration or replacement. With adequate maintenance, the entire instrument suite should be replaced or completely refurbished about once every five to seven years.

Simple preventative maintenance is effective but requires much planning and skilled technical staff. Changes in technology and products require retraining and continual re-education. Travel, logistics, scheduling, and seasonal access restrictions consume major amounts of time and budget but are absolutely necessary. Without such attention, data gradually become less credible and then often are misused or not used at all.

1.4.4. Automated versus Manual Stations
Historic stations often have depended on manual observations and many continue to operate in this mode. Manual observations frequently produce excellent data sets. Sensors and data are simple and intuitive, well tested, and relatively cheap. Manual stations have much to offer in certain circumstances and can be a source of both primary and backup data. However, methodological consistency for manual measurements is a constant challenge, especially with a mobile work force. Operating manual stations takes time and needs to be done on a regular schedule, though sometimes the routine is welcome.

Nearly all newer stations are automated. Automated stations provide better time resolution, increased (though imperfect) reliability, greater capacity for data storage, and improved accessibility to large amounts of data. The purchase cost for automated stations is higher than for manual stations. A common expectation and serious misconception is that an automated station can be deployed and left to operate on its own. In reality, automation does not eliminate the need for people but rather changes the type of person that is needed. Skilled technical personnel are needed and must be readily available, especially if live communications exist and data gaps are not wanted. Site visits are needed at least annually and spare parts must be maintained. Typical annual costs for sensors and maintenance are $1500–2500 per station per year.

6

1.4.5. Communications

With manual stations, the observer is responsible for recording and transmitting station data. Data from automated stations, however, can be transmitted quickly for access by research and operations personnel, which is a highly preferable situation. A comparison of communication systems for automated and manual stations shows that automated stations generally require additional equipment, more power, higher transmission costs, attention to sources of disruption or garbling, and backup procedures (e.g. manual downloads from data loggers).

Automated stations are capable of functioning normally without communication and retaining many months of data. At such sites, however, alerts about station problems are not possible, large gaps can accrue when accessible stations quit, and the constituencies needed to support such stations are smaller and less vocal. Two-way communications permit full recovery from disruptions, ability to reprogram data loggers remotely, and better opportunities for diagnostics and troubleshooting. In virtually all cases, two-way communications are much preferred to all other communication methods. However, two-way communications require considerations of cost, signal access, transmission rates, interference, and methods for keeping sensor and communication power loops separate. Two-way communications are frequently impossible (no service) or impractical, expensive, or power consumptive. Two-way methods (cellular, land line, radio, Internet) require smaller up-front costs as compared to other methods of communication and have variable recurrent costs, starting at zero. Satellite links work everywhere (except when blocked by trees or cliffs) and are quite reliable but are one-way and relatively slow, allow no re-transmissions, and require high up-front costs ($3000-4000) but no recurrent costs. Communications technology is changing constantly and requires vigilant attention by maintenance personnel.

1.4.6. Quality Assurance and Quality Control

Quality control and quality assurance are issues at every step through the entire sequence of sensing, communication, storage, retrieval, and display of environmental data. Quality assurance is an umbrella concept that covers all data collection and processing (start-to-finish) and ensures that credible information is available to the end user. Quality control has a more limited scope and is defined by the International Standards Organization as "the operational techniques and activities that are used to satisfy quality requirements." The central problem can be better appreciated if we approach quality control in the following way.

- Quality control is the evaluation, assessment, and rehabilitation of imperfect data by utilizing other imperfect data.

The quality of the data only decreases with time once the observation is made. The best and most effective quality control, therefore, consists in making high-quality measurements from the start and then successfully transmitting the measurements to an ingest process and storage site. Once the data are received from a monitoring station, a series of checks with increasing complexity can be applied, ranging from single-element checks (self-consistency) to multiple-element checks (inter-sensor consistency) to multiple-station/single-element checks (inter-station consistency). Suitable ancillary data (battery voltages, data ranges for all measurements, etc.) can prove extremely useful in diagnosing problems.

There is rarely a single technique in quality control procedures that will work satisfactorily for all situations. Quality-control procedures must be tailored to individual station circumstances, data access and storage methods, and climate regimes.

The fundamental issue in quality control centers on the tradeoff between falsely rejecting good data (Type I error) and falsely accepting bad data (Type II error). We cannot reduce the incidence of one type of error without increasing the incidence of the other type. In weather and climate data assessments, since good data are absolutely crucial for interpreting climate records properly, Type I errors are deemed far less desirable than Type II errors.

Not all observations are equal in importance. Quality-control procedures are likely to have the greatest difficulty evaluating the most extreme observations, where independent information usually must be sought and incorporated. Quality-control procedures involving more than one station usually involve a great deal of infrastructure with its own (imperfect) error-detection methods, which must be in place before a single value can be evaluated.

1.4.7. Standards
Although there is near-universal recognition of the value in systematic weather and climate measurements, these measurements will have little value unless they conform to accepted standards. There is not a single source for standards for collecting weather and climate data nor a single standard that meets all needs. Measurement standards have been developed by the American Association of State Climatologists (AASC 1985), U.S. Environmental Protection Agency (EPA 1987), World Meteorological Organization (WMO 1983; 2005), Finklin and Fischer (1990), National Wildfire Coordinating Group (2004), and the RAWS program (Bureau of Land Management [BLM] 1997). Variations to these measurement standards also have been offered by instrument makers (e.g., Tanner 1990).

1.4.8. Who Makes the Measurements?
The lands under NPS stewardship provide many excellent locations to host the monitoring of climate by the NPS or other collaborators. These lands are largely protected from human development and other land changes that can impact observed climate records. Most park units historically have observed weather/climate elements as part of their overall mission. Many of these measurements come from station networks managed by other agencies, with observations taken or overseen by NPS personnel, in some cases, or by collaborators from the other agencies. National Park Service units that are small, lack sufficient resources, or lack sites presenting adequate exposure may benefit by utilizing weather/climate measurements collected from nearly stations.

2.0. Climate Background

Climate is a key driver of natural systems that affects system structure, composition, and function. Climate data can provide a background explanation for changes or variation in other vital signs. Measures of climate such as precipitation and temperature are critical to understanding the ecological condition of aquatic and terrestrial resources and biota (Hynes 1975; Poff 1997). Monitoring basic climate variables will provide a long-term record of the stress associated with climate change. While management applications related to climate are limited, climate data are useful for ruling out other causes for system responses. It is therefore essential to understand the climate characteristics of the NETN. These characteristics are discussed in this chapter.

2.1. Climate and the NETN Environment

The NETN is located within the temperate deciduous forest biome (Shriver et al. 2005). Historically, the temperate deciduous forest biome has undergone some of the greatest human disturbance of any major biome (Hannah et al. 1995). These disturbances include the removal of native forests for timber and agriculture, and urban development. These disturbances directly influence the local climate characteristics at each of the NETN parks and also influence region-wide climate changes in the NETN. Road construction and maintenance activities are among the most common types of disturbances in the NETN (Trombulak and Frissell 2000; Shriver et al. 2005).

As a result of human stresses, the natural systems of the NETN are likely becoming more susceptible to extreme storm events. Common types of storm events include ice storms and nor'easters, which usually occur from fall to spring. Nor'easters are strong low-pressure centers that develop along the Atlantic Ocean's Gulf Stream current and move northeastward along the east coast of the U.S. Ice storms are known to be a primary disturbance mechanism for the hardwood temperate forests in eastern North America, including the NETN (Irland 1998; Pasher and King 2006). Ice storms in the U.S. occur most commonly in the northeast, including the NETN (Changnon 2003; Changnon and Karl 2003). Moderate to severe ice storms have occurred several times in the NETN in the last few decades (Irland 1998; DeGaetano 2000; Changnon 2003). These storms are known to cause significant disturbances to forest canopies, which can both benefit understory growth (increased sunlight) and also inhibit it due to woody debris deposition (Kraft et al. 2002; Darwin et al. 2004; Millward and Kraft 2004; Pasher and King 2006). One of the most severe ice storms in recent memory occurred in January, 1998. This storm damaged millions of hectares of forests in the northeastern U.S. and southeastern Canada (Irland 1998; DeGaetano 2000; Millward and Kraft 2004). Some damaged forests in the NETN required several years to recover fully from the 1998 ice storm (Darwin et al. 2004).

Occasionally, tropical storms or hurricanes or the remnants thereof impact the NETN during the summer and fall seasons. Like ice storms, these can significantly alter the structure and composition of the forests in the NETN (Boose et al. 2001). In some rare instances during the fall months, tropical systems have combined with extratropical low pressure centers to create exceptionally strong nor'easter storms. An example of this is the well-known "Perfect Storm" in October, 1991, where an extratropical low combined with energy from Hurricane Grace to create a very powerful nor'easter.

Although these extreme storm events can be beneficial to natural systems, they often cause or magnify disturbances which make plant and animal communities more susceptible to diseases and insect infestations. They also introduce further habitat fragmentation in areas that are already significantly fragmented by human uses.

Climate change is expected to have substantial long-term impacts at all NETN park units, especially along the coastal and high-elevation ecosystems of the NETN (Shriver et al. 2005). Climate change is both directly and indirectly altering many key environmental parameters that control the structure, composition and function of ecosystems. While accurate prediction of the effects of the suite of global change stressors upon ecosystems is currently beyond our abilities, a large body of research has been assembled which yields some insight into what may occur. A growing body of evidence also indicates that human activities have accelerated the concentration of greenhouse gases in the atmosphere (IPCC 2002). The climate of the northeastern United Sates is projected to become warmer and perhaps wetter over the next 100 years (New England Regional Assessment Group 2001), changes that will likely affect the structure and function of all ecosystems. Elevated CO_2 has been shown to increase photosynthetic rates and tree growth, though this may be a short-term effect (Long et al. 1996; Rey and Jarvis 1998) that is likely to be limited under field conditions by nutrient availability (Curtis and Wang 1998; Johnson et al. 1998).

Several studies indicate that spring is coming earlier in the NETN. The annual date of the last hard spring freeze shifted significantly earlier between 1961 and 1990 (Cooter and Leduc 1995) and lilac bloom dates at four stations shifted significantly earlier between 1959 and 1993 (Schwartz and Reiter 2000). The impacts of climate change on hydrology in the NETN are just beginning to be understood. Much of the significant change towards earlier lake ice-out dates in New England since the 1800s occurred from 1968 to 2000 (Hodgkins et al. 2003). All of 11 studied rivers in New England had significantly earlier winter/spring high flows from earlier snowmelt, with most of the change occurring in the last 30 years (Hodgkins et al. 2003). Furthermore, snow density on or near March 1 has significantly increased in coastal Maine over the last 60 years, indicating earlier spring melting (Dudley and Hodgkins 2002).

Projected increases in temperature would increase the rate of evapotranspiration, which in turn could alter wetland hydrology. Hydrologic alterations that reduced the flooding period would have the most negative impacts on ephemeral wetland or vernal pools (Brooks 2004). Changes in wetland water temperature due to rapidly changing climate are expected to affect the characteristics of wetland fauna populations in the NETN (Root and Schneider 2002). Wetland ecosystems are thought to be especially sensitive to climate changes because of the synergistic effects of habitat fragmentation and the increased need for dispersal of wetland fauna caused by a reduction in habitat quality. The increasingly urbanized landscapes in the NETN are becoming more hostile to dispersing wetland fauna, further restricting the ability of wetland ecosystems to respond to climate changes (Gibbs and Shriver 2002; Steen and Gibbs 2004).

2.2. Spatial Variability
Topography and proximity to the Atlantic Ocean both exert an influence on the overall climate characteristics of the NETN. North-south gradients are present in the NETN for precipitation

(see Figures 2.1 and 2.2). The drier locations in the NETN are generally located in lower-elevation interior areas such as the Champlain Valley, where mean annual precipitation is often below 1000 mm. The driest park units in the NETN, SAGA and SARA, are each located in interior valley locations and receive on average just under 1000 mm per year. Locations closer to the Atlantic generally receive more precipitation, with mean annual precipitation totals that approach 1400 mm. The wettest park units in the NETN are ACAD, MORR, and WEFA, and they are all located nearer to the Atlantic coast. The wettest parts of the NETN region as a whole are the higher elevations, including the southern Adirondack Mountains in New York, the White Mountains in New Hampshire, and the Green Mountains in Vermont. Mount Washington, located in the White Mountains, is the wettest location in the NETN. This location receives over 2000 mm of precipitation every year, on average. Much of the precipitation in the NETN is associated with strong low-pressure centers that develop along the Atlantic Ocean's Gulf Stream current and move northeastward along the east coast of the U.S. Precipitation totals with the stronger storms can easily exceed 100 mm. Local topography provides orographic enhancement of the precipitation in the higher elevations of the NETN, especially on south- and west-facing slopes. Convective processes contribute a small portion of the precipitation during the spring and summer months. While almost all of the yearly precipitation is rainfall for areas near the coast, snowfall constitutes a significant proportion of the yearly precipitation in interior portions of the NETN (see Figure 2.2). Strong nor'easter events contribute much of this snowfall. Annual snowfall totals in the interior locations of the NETN can reach 800 cm at the highest elevations such as Mount Washington.

Precipitation occurs regularly throughout the year in the NETN (Shriver et al. 2005). However, there are noteworthy seasonal variations. More precipitation appears to fall in the winter months in the northern/eastern portions of the NETN, such as Maine, while more precipitation falls during the summer months in the southern/western portions of the NETN, such as New Jersey (Figure 2.3).

As with precipitation, there are north-south gradients in temperature across the NETN (Figure 2.4). Mean annual temperatures in the NETN range from under 1°C in portions of northwestern Maine, to greater than 11°C in New Jersey and southern New York. The coolest park unit in the NETN is MABI, where the mean annual temperature is around 5°C. The warmest park units are MORR and WEFA, where the mean annual temperatures are at or just above 9°C.

Temperatures vary greatly throughout the year in the NETN. This region is exposed to both polar and subtropical air masses throughout the year and receives four distinct seasons (Shriver et al. 2005). January minimum temperatures in the NETN are generally between -5°C and -10°C along the Atlantic coast but commonly get below -20°C in northern Maine (Figure 2.5). The average January minimum temperatures at MABI are the coldest in the NETN, averaging around -17°C. In fact, winter minimum temperatures have gotten as cold as -40°C near MABI and SAGA, along the Connecticut River Valley in Vermont and New Hampshire. July maximum temperatures, on the other hand, can get quite warm (Figure 2.6). The warmest average July maximum temperatures in the NETN occur in northern New Jersey, reaching up to 30°C. Summer temperatures in this region have been as high as 40°C. Higher elevations are still relatively cool in July, with average maximum temperatures at or just above 20°C.

11

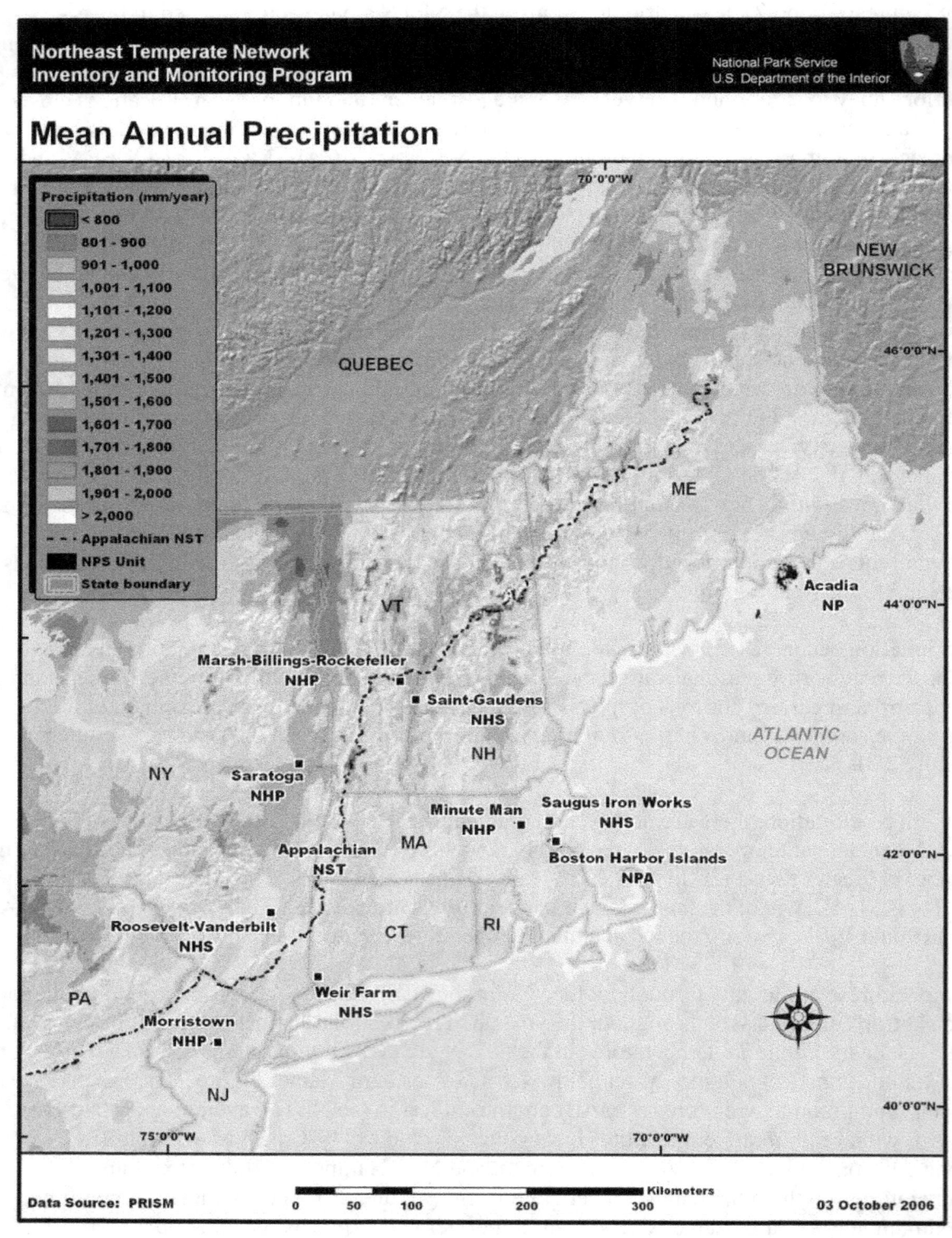

Figure 2.1. Mean annual precipitation, 1961-1990, for the NETN.

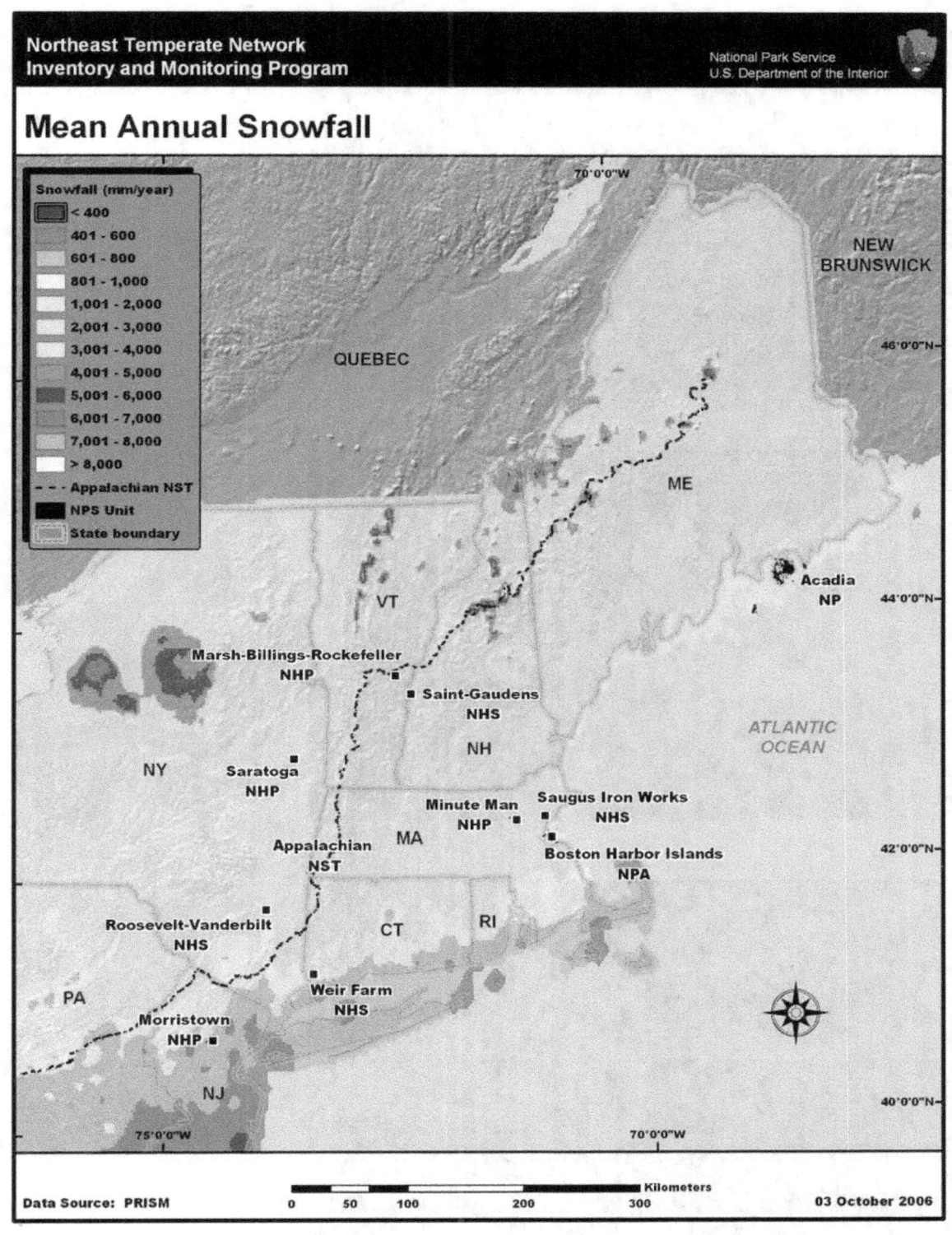

Figure 2.2. Mean annual snowfall, 1961-1990, for the NETN.

a)

b)

c)

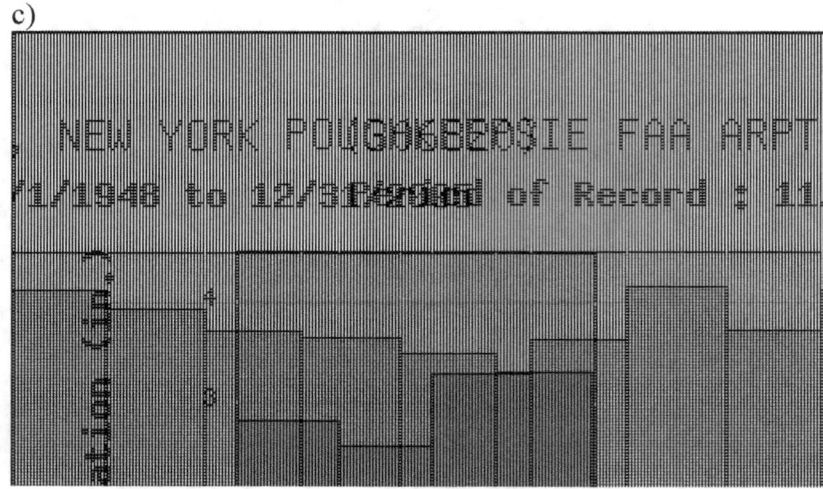

Figure 2.3. Mean monthly precipitation at selected locations in the NETN. Jonesboro, Maine, near ACAD (a); Boston, Massachusetts (b); and at Poughkeepsie, New York, near ROVA (c).

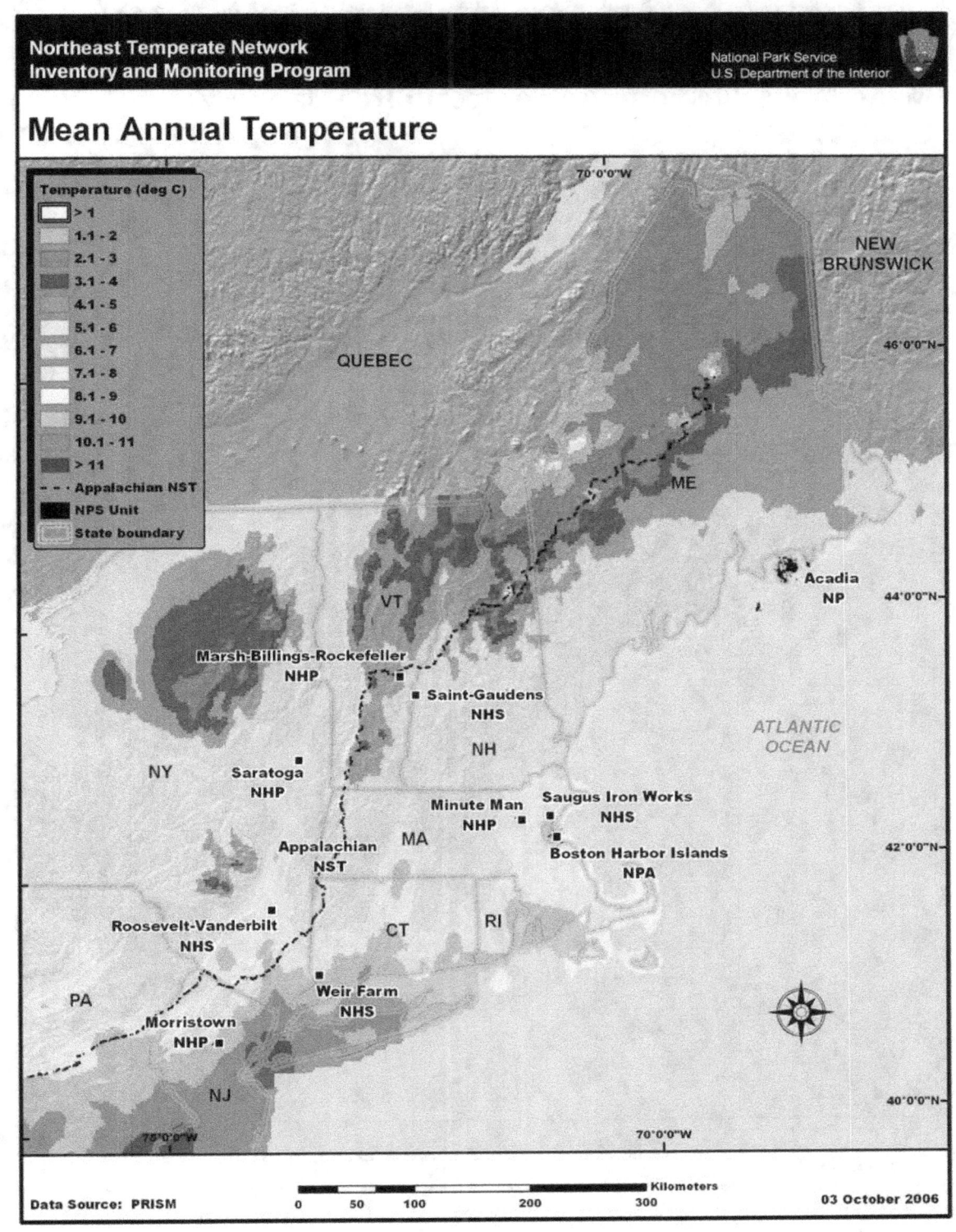

Figure 2.4. Mean annual temperature, 1961-1990, for the NETN.

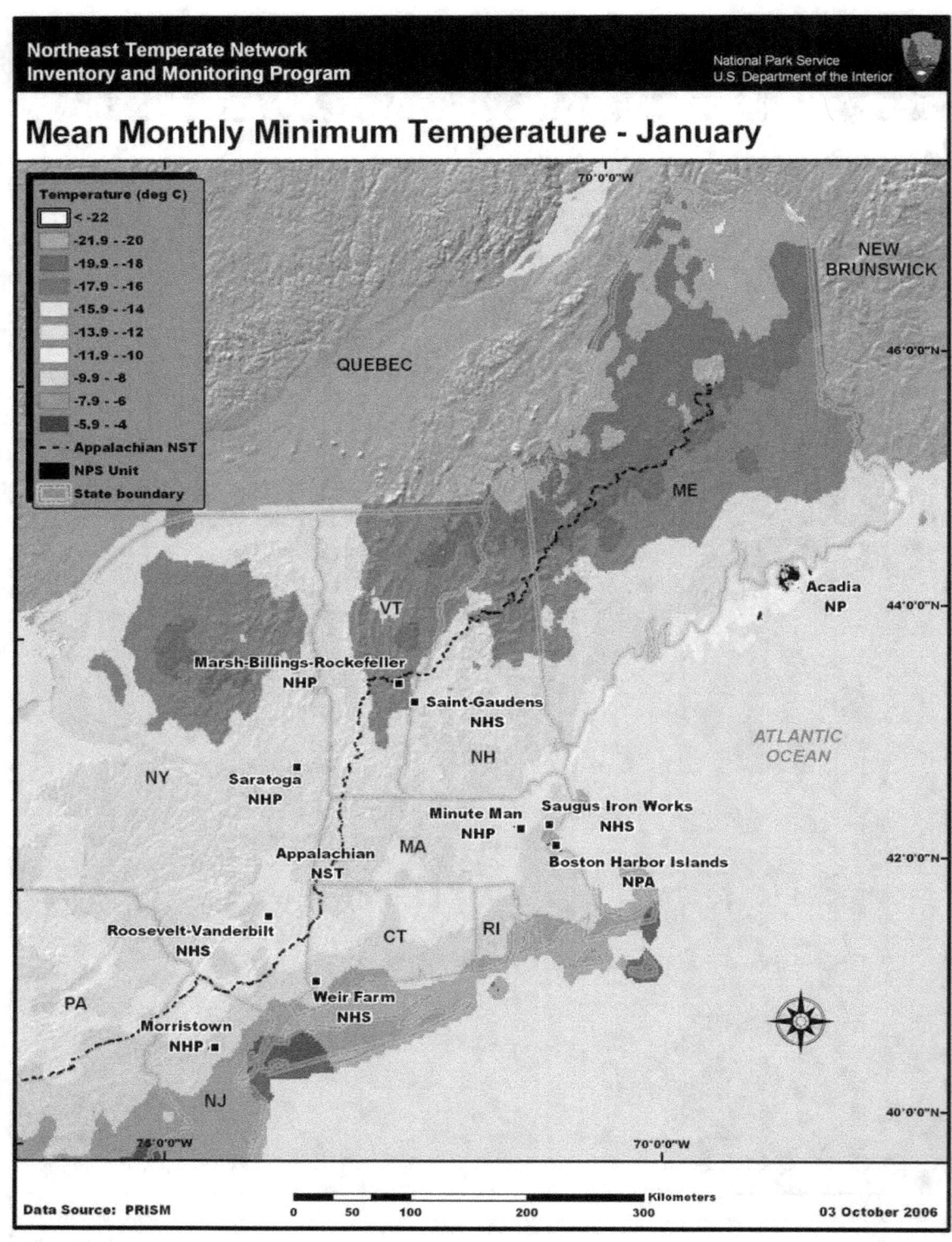

Figure 2.5. Mean January minimum temperature, 1961-1990, for the NETN.

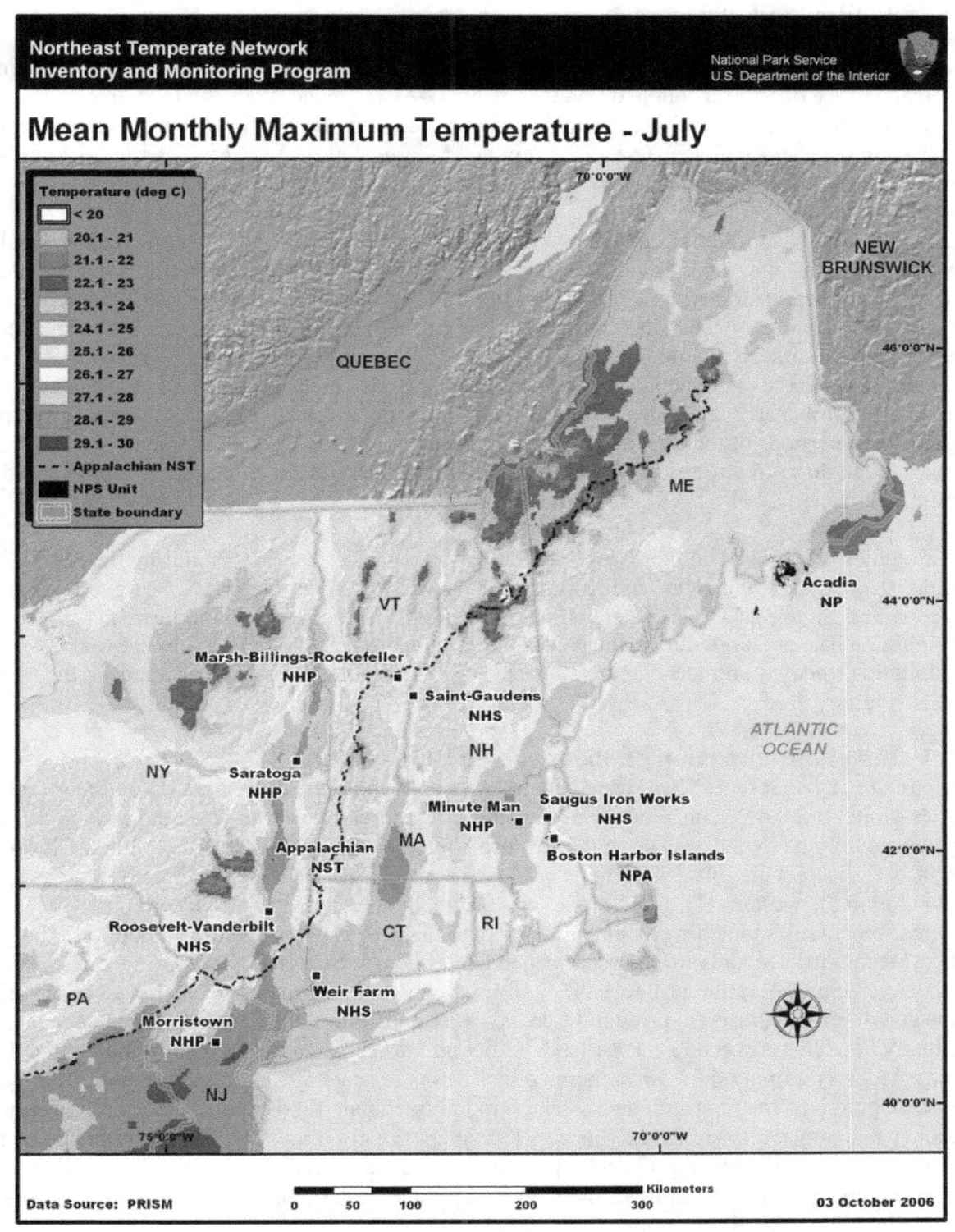

Figure 2.6. Mean July maximum temperature, 1961-1990, for the NETN.

2.3. Temporal Variability

The North Atlantic Oscillation – Arctic Oscillation (NAO-AO) is a major source of low-frequency climate variability in eastern North America (Hurrell 1995), with NAO-AO variations occurring on the order of a couple decades. The NAO-AO influences heavily the wintertime temperature characteristics of the northeastern U.S., including the NETN (Hurrell and van Loon 1997; Thompson and Wallace 1998; Wettstein and Mearns 2002). Warmer winter temperatures occur in eastern North America when the NAO-AO index is positive.

The number and severity of storm events in the NETN varies greatly from year to year. Several nor'easters of varying intensities impact the NETN region each year. Other storm events are not as frequent. Moderate to severe ice storms occur in the NETN region once or twice a decade (Irland 1998; Changnon 2003). It is thought that one of the results of future climate changes in the eastern U.S. may be an increase in the number of ice storms (NAST 2001). There may also be significant changes in the number and intensity of extreme events such as hurricanes and nor'easters (Groisman et al. 2000). Currently, the numbers of tropical cyclones that reach central and northern portions of the U.S. east coast are quite sporadic but the events, when they do occur, tend to do so in clusters. These clusters of storms occur on time scales of a couple decades (Smith 1999).

Some studies have observed increases in precipitation over the eastern U.S. during the last century (Karl et al. 1996b; Karl and Knight 1998; NAST 2001). In the NETN, however, this is not apparent (Figure 2.7). Some regions, such as central Massachusetts, do indicate that precipitation has increased during the past century; however, most other regions show no precipitation trends. Long-term temperature time series do not show any clear trends in the NETN (Figure 2.8).

2.4. Parameter Regression on Independent Slopes Model

The climate maps presented here were generated using the Parameter Regression on Independent Slopes Model (PRISM). This model was developed to address the extreme spatial and elevation gradients exhibited by the climate of the western United States (Daly et al. 1994; 2002; Gibson et al. 2002; Doggett et al. 2004). The maps produced through PRISM have undergone rigorous evaluation in the western U.S. This model was originally developed to provide climate information at scales matching available land-cover maps to assist in ecologic modeling. The PRISM technique accounts for the scale-dependent effects of topography on mean values of climate elements. Elevation provides the first-order constraint for the mapped climate fields, with slope and orientation (aspect) providing second-order constraints. The model has been enhanced gradually to address inversions, coast/land gradients, and climate patterns in small-scale trapping basins. Monthly climate fields are generated by PRISM to account for seasonal variations in elevation gradients in climate elements. These monthly climate fields then can be combined into seasonal and annual climate fields. Since PRISM maps are grid maps, they do not replicate point values but rather, for a given grid cell, represent the grid-cell average of the climate variable in question at the average elevation for that cell. The model relies on observed surface and upper-air measurements to estimate spatial climate fields.

a)

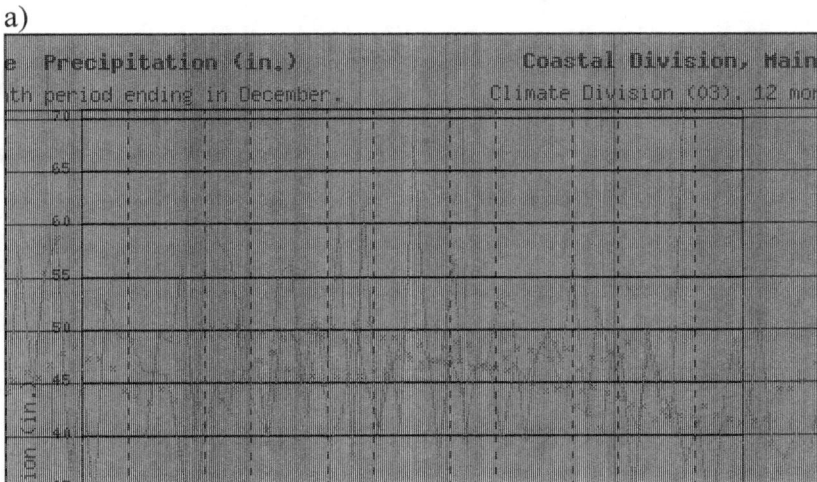

e Precipitation (in.)   Coastal Division, Main
th period ending in December.   Climate Division (03). 12 mo

b)

setts Precipitation (in.)   Central Division, Massachu
th period ending in December.   Climate Division (02). 12 mo

c)

rsey Precipitation (in.)   Northern Division, New Je
th period ending in December.   Climate Division (01). 12 mo

Figure 2.7. Precipitation time series, 1895-2005, for selected regions in the NETN. These include twelve-month precipitation (ending in December) (red), 10-year running mean (blue), mean (green), and plus/minus one standard deviation (green dotted). Locations include coastal Maine (a), central Massachusetts (b), and northern New Jersey (c).

a)

b)

c)

Figure 2.8. Temperature time series, 1895-2005, for selected regions in the NETN. These include twelve-month average temperature (ending in December) (red), 10-year running mean (blue), mean (green), and plus/minus one standard deviation (green dotted). Locations include coastal Maine (a), central Massachusetts (b), and northern New Jersey (c).

3.0. Methods

Having discussed the climatic characteristics of the NETN, we now present the procedures that were used to obtain information for weather/climate stations within the NETN. This information was obtained from various sources, as mentioned in the following paragraphs. Retrieval of station metadata constituted a major component of this work.

3.1. Metadata Retrieval

A key component of station inventories is determining the kinds of observations that have been conducted over time, by whom, and in what manner; when each type of observation began and ended; and whether these observations are still being conducted. Metadata about the observational process (Table 3.1) generally consist of a series of vignettes that apply to time intervals and, therefore, constitute a *history* rather than a single snapshot. An expanded list of relevant metadata fields for this inventory is provided in Appendix F. This report has relied on metadata records from three sources: (a) Western Regional Climate Center (WRCC), (b) NPS personnel, and (c) other knowledgeable personnel, such as state climate office staff.

The initial metadata sources for this report were stored at WRCC. This regional climate center (RCC) acts as a working repository of many western climate records, including the main networks outlined in this section. The WRCC conducts live and periodic data collection (ingests) from all major national and western weather/climate networks. These networks include the COOP network, the Surface Airways Observations Network (SAO) operated by NWS and the Federal Aviation Administration (FAA), the interagency RAWS network, and various smaller networks. The WRCC is expanding its capability to ingest information from other networks as resources permit and usefulness dictates. This center has relied heavily on historic archives (in many cases supplemented with live ingests) to assess the quantity (not necessarily quality) of data available for NPS I&M network applications.

The primary source of metadata at WRCC is the Applied Climate Information System (ACIS), a joint effort among RCCs and other NOAA entities. Metadata for NETN weather/climate stations identified from the ACIS database are available in file "NETN_from_ACIS.tar.gz" (see Appendix G). Historic metadata pertaining to major climate- and weather-observing systems in the U.S. are stored in ACIS where metadata are linked to the observed data. A distributed system, ACIS is synchronized among the RCCs. Mainstream software is utilized, including Postgress, Python™, and Java™ programming languages; CORBA®-compliant network software; and industry-standard, nonproprietary hardware and software. Metadata and data for all major national climate and weather networks have been entered into the ACIS database. For this project, the available metadata from many smaller networks also have been entered but in most cases the actual data have not yet been entered. Data sets are in the NetCDF (Network Common Data Form) format, but the design allows for integration with legacy systems, including non-NetCDF files (used at WRCC) and additional metadata (added for this project). The ACIS also supports a suite of products to visualize or summarize data from these data sets. National climate-monitoring maps are updated daily using the ACIS data feed. The developmental phases of ACIS have utilized metadata supplied by the NCDC and NWS with many tens of thousands of entries, screened as well as possible for duplications, mistakes, and omissions.

Table 3.1. Primary metadata fields for NETN weather/climate stations. Explanations are provided as appropriate.

Metadata Field	Notes
Station name	Station name associated with network listed in "Climate Network."
Latitude	Numerical value (units: see coordinate units).
Longitude	Numerical value (units: see coordinate units).
Coordinate units	Latitude/longitude (units: decimal degrees, degree-minute-second, etc.).
Datum	Datum used as basis for coordinates: WGS 84, NAD 83, etc.
Elevation	Elevation of station above mean sea level (m).
Slope	Slope of ground surface below station (degrees).
Aspect	Azimuth that ground surface below station faces.
Climate division	NOAA climate division where station is located. Climate divisions are NOAA-specified zones sharing similar climate and hydrology characteristics.
Country	Country where station is located.
State	State where station is located.
County	County where station is located.
Weather/climate network	Primary weather/climate network the station belongs to (RAWS, Clean Air Status and Trends Network [CASTNet], etc.).
NPS unit code	Four-letter code identifying park unit where station resides.
NPS unit name	Full name of park unit.
NPS unit type	National park, national monument, etc.
UTM zone	If UTM is the only coordinate system available.
Location notes	Useful information not already included in "station narrative."
Climate variables	Temperature, precipitation, etc.
Installation date	Date of station installation.
Removal date	Date of station removal.
Station photograph	Digital image of station.
Photograph date	Date photograph was taken.
Photographer	Name of person who took the photograph.
Station narrative	Anything related to general site description; may include site exposure, characteristics of surrounding vegetation, driving directions, etc.
Contact name	Name of the person involved with station operation.
Organization	Group or agency affiliation of contact person.
Contact type	Designation that identifies contact person as the station owner, observer, maintenance person, data manager, etc.
Position/job title	Official position/job title of contact person.
Address	Address of contact person.
E-mail address	E-mail address of contact person.
Phone	Phone number of contact person (and extension if available).
Contact notes	Other information needed to reach contact person.

In addition to obtaining NETN weather/climate station metadata from ACIS, metadata were obtained from NPS staff at the NETN office in Woodstock, Vermont. The metadata provided from the NETN office are available in file "NETN_NPS.tar.gz." Most of the stations noted by NETN staff are already accounted for in ACIS. In addition, we have relied on information

22

supplied at various times in the past by NCDC and the Northeast Regional Climate Center (NERCC), along with the state climate office of New Jersey (Table 3.2).

Table 3.2. Additional sources of weather and climate metadata for the NETN.

Name	Position	Phone Number	Email Address
Keith Eggleston	Research Support, NERCC	(607)255-1749	kle1@cornell.edu
David Robinson	New Jersey State Climatologist	(732)445-4741	drobins@rci.rutgers.edu

Two types of information have been used to complete the climate station inventory for NETN.

- Station inventories: Information about observational procedures, latitude/longitude, elevation, measured elements, measurement frequency, sensor types, exposures, ground cover and vegetation, data-processing details, network, purpose, and managing individual or agency, etc.

- Data inventories: Information about measured data values including completeness, seasonality, data gaps, representation of missing data, flagging systems, how special circumstances in the data record are denoted, etc.

This is not a straightforward process. Extensive searches are typically required to develop historic station and data inventories. Both types of inventories frequently contain information gaps and often rely on tacit and unrealistic assumptions. Sources of information for these inventories frequently are difficult to recover or are undocumented and unreliable. In many cases, the actual weather/climate data available from different sources are not linked directly to metadata records. To the extent that actual data can be acquired (rather than just metadata), it is possible to cross-check these records and perform additional assessments based on the amount and completeness of the data.

Certain types of weather/climate networks that possess any of the following attributes have not been considered for inclusion in the inventory:

- Private networks with proprietary access and/or inability to obtain or provide sufficient metadata.
- Private weather enthusiasts (often with high-quality data) whose metadata are not available and whose data are not readily accessible.
- Unofficial observers supplying data to the NWS (lack of access to current data and historic archives; lack of metadata).
- Networks having no available historic data.
- Networks having poor-quality metadata.
- Networks having poor access to metadata.
- Real-time networks having poor access to real-time data.

Previous inventory efforts at WRCC have shown that for the weather networks identified in the preceding list, in light of the need for quality data to track weather and climate, the resources required and difficulty encountered in obtaining metadata or data are prohibitively large.

3.2. Criteria for Locating Stations

To identify stations for each park unit in NETN, we selected only those that were located within a specified buffer distance of the NETN park units. This buffer distance was 10 km for BOHA, MIMA, MORR, and SAIR, due to their urban settings in the Boston and New York metropolitan areas. For all other NETN parks, this buffer distance was set at 40 km. We selected these buffer distances in an attempt to include at least a few automated stations from major networks such as SAO. We also chose these buffer distances in an attempt to keep the size of the stations lists under 500 stations per park unit.

The station locator maps presented in Chapter 4 were designed to show clearly the spatial distributions of all major weather/climate station networks in NETN. We recognize that other mapping formats may be more suitable for other specific needs.

4.0. Station Inventory

An objective of this report is to show the locations of weather/climate stations for the NETN region in relation to the boundaries of the NPS park units within the NETN. A station does not have to be within park boundaries to provide useful data and information for a park unit.

4.1. Climate and Weather Networks

Most stations in the NETN region are associated with at least one of eight major weather/climate networks (Table 4.1). Brief descriptions of each weather/climate network are provided below (see Appendix H for greater detail).

Table 4.1. Weather/climate networks represented within the NETN.

Acronym	Name
CASTNet	Clean Air Status and Trends Network
COOP	NWS Cooperative Observer Program
CWOP	Citizen Weather Observer Program
GPMP	Gaseous Pollutant Monitoring Program
GPS-MET	NOAA ground-based GPS meteorology
RAWS	Remote Automated Weather Station network
SAO	NWS/FAA Surface Airways Observation network
WX4U	Weather For You network

4.1.1. Clean Air Status and Trends Network (CASTNet)

CASTNet is primarily an air-quality monitoring network managed by the EPA. Standard hourly weather and climate elements are measured and include temperature, wind, humidity, solar radiation, soil temperature, and sometimes moisture. These elements are intended to support interpretation of air-quality parameters that also are measured at CASTNet sites. Data records at CASTNet sites are generally one–two decades in length.

4.1.2. NWS Cooperative Observer Program (COOP)

The COOP network has been a foundation of the U.S. climate program for decades and continues to play an important role. Manual measurements are made by volunteers and consist of daily maximum and minimum temperatures, temperature at the time of observation, daily precipitation, daily snowfall, and snow depth. When blended with NWS measurements, the data set is known as SOD, or "Summary of the Day." The quality of data from COOP sites ranges from excellent to modest.

4.1.3. Citizen Weather Observer Program (CWOP)

The CWOP network consists primarily of automated weather stations operated by private citizens who have either an Internet connection and/or a wireless Ham radio setup. Data from CWOP stations are specifically intended for use in research, education, and homeland security activities. Although meteorological elements such as temperature, precipitation, and wind are measured at all CWOP stations, station characteristics do vary, including sensor types and site exposure.

4.1.4. Gaseous Pollutant Monitoring Program (GPMP)

The GPMP network measures hourly meteorological data in support of pollutant monitoring activities. Measured elements include temperature, precipitation, humidity, wind, solar radiation, and surface wetness. These data are generally of high quality, with records extending up to 1-2 decades in length.

4.1.5. NOAA Ground-Based GPS Meteorology (GPS-MET)

The GPS-MET network is the first network of its kind dedicated to GPS meteorology (see Duan et al. 1996). GPS meteorology utilizes the radio signals broadcast by the satellite Global Positioning System for atmospheric remote sensing. GPS meteorology applications have evolved along two paths: ground-based (Bevis et al. 1992) and space-based (Yuan et al. 1993). For more information, please see Appendix G. The stations identified in this inventory are all ground-based. The GPS-MET network was developed in response to the need for improved moisture observations to support weather forecasting, climate monitoring, and other research activities. The primary goals of this network are to measure atmospheric water vapor using ground-based GPS receivers, facilitate the operational use of these data, and encourage usage of GPS meteorology for atmospheric research and other applications. GPS-MET is a collaboration between NOAA and several other governmental and university organizations and institutions. Ancillary meteorological observations at GPS-MET stations include temperature, relative humidity, and pressure.

4.1.6. Remote Automated Weather Station Network (RAWS)

The RAWS network is administered through many land management agencies, particularly the BLM and the Forest Service. Hourly meteorology elements are measured and include temperature, wind, humidity, solar radiation, barometric pressure, fuel temperature, and precipitation (when temperatures are above freezing). The fire community is the primary client for RAWS data. These sites are remote and data are typically transmitted via GOES (Geostationary Operational Environmental Satellite). Some sites operate all winter. Most data records for RAWS sites began during or after the mid-1980s.

4.1.7. NWS/FAA Surface Airways Observation Network (SAO)

These stations are located usually at major airports and military bases. Almost all SAO sites are automated. The hourly data measured at these sites include temperature, precipitation, humidity, wind, pressure, sky cover, ceiling, visibility, and current weather. Most data records begin during or after the 1940s, and these data are generally of high quality.

4.1.8. Weather For You Network (WX4U)

The WX4U network is a nationwide collection of weather stations run by local observers. Data quality varies with site. Standard meteorological elements are measured and usually include temperature, precipitation, wind, and humidity.

4.1.9. Weather Bureau Army Navy (WBAN)

This is a station identification system rather than a true weather/climate network and is not discussed in Appendix H. A brief description of WBAN is provided here. Stations identified with WBAN are largely historical stations that reported meteorological observations on the WBAN weather observation forms that were common during the early and middle parts of the 20th Century. However, some stations identified with WBAN are operating currently. The use of WBAN numbers to identify stations was one of the first attempts in the U.S. to use a coordinated station numbering scheme between several weather station networks, such as the SAO and COOP networks.

4.1.10. Other Networks
In addition to the major networks mentioned above, there are various networks that are operated for specific purposes by specific organizations or governmental agencies or scientific research projects. These networks could be present within NETN but have not been identified in this report. Some of the commonly used networks include the following:

- NOAA upper-air stations
- National Atmospheric Deposition Program (NADP)
- Federal and state departments of transportation
- National Science Foundation Long-Term Ecologic Research Network
- U.S. Department of Energy Surface Radiation Budget Network (Surfrad)
- U.S. Geological Survey (USGS) hydrologic stations
- Park-specific-monitoring networks and stations
- Other research or project networks having many possible owners

4.2. Station Locations
The major weather/climate networks in the NETN (discussed in Section 4.1) have at most a few stations that are at or inside each park unit (Table 4.2). Acadia National Park has the most weather/climate stations located inside park boundaries (four). In all, we have identified five weather/climate stations inside the park units of the NETN.

Lists of stations have been compiled for the NETN. A station does not have to be within the boundaries to provide useful data and information regarding the park unit in question. Some might be physically *within* the administrative or political boundaries, whereas others might be just outside, or even some distance away, but would be *nearby* in behavior and representativeness. What constitutes "useful" and "representative" are also significant questions, whose answers can vary according to application, type of element, period of record, procedural or methodological observation conventions, and the like.

4.2.1. Northern Park Units
Only two park units in the NETN have weather/climate stations located inside park boundaries. These two park units, ACAD and SARA, are both located in the northern part of the NETN (Table 4.3; Figure 4.1). One weather/climate station has been located in SARA, while four weather/climate stations have been identified in ACAD.

Table 4.2. Number of stations within or nearby NETN park units. Numbers are listed by park unit and by weather/climate network. Figures in parentheses indicate the numbers of stations within park boundaries.

Network	ACAD	BOHA	MABI	MIMA	MORR
CASTNet	1(0)	0(0)	0(0)	0(0)	0(0)
COOP	6(1)	16(0)	29(0)	15(0)	5(0)
CWOP	1(0)	24(0)	2(0)	24(0)	5(0)
GPMP	3(2)	0(0)	0(0)	0(0)	0(0)
GPS-MET	2(0)	0(0)	0(0)	0(0)	0(0)
RAWS	2(0)	0(0)	0(0)	0(0)	0(0)
SAO	6(0)	4(0)	2(0)	3(0)	0(0)
WX4U	0(0)	2(0)	0(0)	2(0)	0(0)
Other	4(1)	1(0)	1(0)	1(0)	1(0)
Total	25(4)	47(0)	34(0)	45(0)	11(0)
Network	**ROVA**	**SAGA**	**SAIR**	**SARA**	**WEFA**
CASTNet	0(0)	0(0)	0(0)	0(0)	0(0)
COOP	24(0)	33(0)	25(0)	17(0)	39(0)
CWOP	10(0)	4(0)	12(0)	25(0)	12(0)
GPMP	0(0)	0(0)	0(0)	0(0)	0(0)
GPS-MET	0(0)	0(0)	0(0)	1(0)	0(0)
RAWS	0(0)	0(0)	1(1)	0(0)	0(0)
SAO	1(0)	2(0)	2(0)	4(0)	3(0)
WX4U	0(0)	0(0)	2(0)	2(0)	3(0)
Other	0(0)	1(0)	0(0)	1(0)	3(0)
Total	35(0)	40(0)	43(1)	49(0)	60(0)

Of the four stations identified within ACAD, two are currently active (Table 4.3). These include a GPMP station (Cadillac Mountain) that has been operating since 1995 and a COOP station (Acadia National Park) that has been operating since 1982. A GPMP site operated at the headquarters of ACAD up until 2000. We have identified 21 stations that are outside but within 30 km of ACAD. Thirteen of these stations are active. Most of the stations we have identified here are located around the eastern park units of ACAD (Figure 4.1) A CASTNet station and a RAWS station are both operating at McFarland Hill, which is just outside of the eastern unit of ACAD on Mount Desert Island. These sites have provided near-real-time weather observations since the late 1990s and early 2000s. The longest periods of record come from the SAO station at Bar Harbor Airport. This station has been operating since 1935 and has a reliable record of data. Five other SAO sites provide near-real-time weather observations within 30 km of ACAD. No weather/climate stations were identified within MABI (Table 4.3). Only 15 of the 34 stations we identified within 30 km of MABI are currently active. All but four of these are COOP stations. The longest COOP records are found from "Hanover" (1884-present), "Woodstock" (1892-present), "Cavendish" (1903-present), and "Newport" (1928-present). The data record at "Hanover" is reliable but has a few data gaps. These gaps occurred in March and April of 1978, September 1978, September 1979, November 1988, December 1996, December 1997, June 2001, and December 2004. The data record at "Cavendish" is the most reliable of these four stations, with the only data gaps occurring in November 1952 and March 2005. The COOP stations "Newport" and "Woodstock" have significant data gaps. "Woodstock" has two major data gaps, one from March 1978 through August 1979 and the other from December 1987 through April 1998. The only reliable data for "Newport" were from August 1991 to present. Two SAO stations have been identified within 30 km of MABI and provide the primary source of near-real-time weather observations for MABI. The longer record, which goes back to 1943, is from the SAO station at Lebanon Municipal Airport.

Like MABI, no weather/climate stations were identified within SAGA (Table 4.3). Of the 40 stations we identified within 30 km of SAGA, 18 are currently active. All but six of these active stations are COOP stations. The long-term COOP records we found for MABI are also applicable for SAGA, since the two park units are only about 10 km apart (Figure 4.1). The two SAO stations identified for MABI also provide near-real-time weather observations for SAGA.

Table 4.3. Weather/climate stations for the northern NETN park units. Stations inside park units and within 30 km of the park unit boundary are included. Missing entries are indicated by "M".

Name	Lat.	Lon.	Elev. (m)	Network	Start	End	In Park?
Acadia National Park (ACAD)							
Acadia National Park	44.374	-68.259	143	COOP	8/1/1982	Present	Yes
Acadia Park HQ GPMP	44.374	-68.262	122	GPMP	10/1/1982	5/1/2000	Yes
Cadillac Mountain	44.347	-68.228	466	GPMP	7/1/1995	Present	Yes
Cadillac Mtn AAF	44.350	-68.233	463	WBAN	10/1/1942	6/30/1944	Yes
McFarland Hill	44.377	-68.261	158	CASTNet	2/1/1998	Present	No
Bar Harbor 3 NW	44.417	-68.250	34	COOP	1/1/1893	8/1/1982	No
Ellsworth	44.533	-68.433	6	COOP	3/23/1910	8/1/1995	No
Ellsworth Poll Control	44.535	-68.421	15	COOP	1/6/2000	Present	No
Lincoln San Dist WTP	44.375	-68.513	52	COOP	11/1/2000	Present	No
Matinicus Rock L B S	43.783	-68.850	9	COOP	3/8/1960	4/1/1974	No
W1UWG Southwest Harbor	44.292	-68.342	40	CWOP	M	Present	No
Acadia Seawall	44.377	-68.261	158	GPMP	4/1/2000	9/1/2001	No
Bar Harbor	44.400	-68.220	31	GPS-MET	M	Present	No
Penobscot	44.450	-68.770	58	GPS-MET	M	Present	No
Isle au Haut	44.067	-68.642	15	RAWS	8/1/1992	12/31/1992	No
McFarland Hill	44.377	-68.261	129	RAWS	4/1/2002	Present	No
Bar Harbor Airport	44.450	-68.367	27	SAO	7/1/1935	Present	No
Bear Island	44.283	-68.267	0	SAO	9/1/1972	Present	No
Egg Rock Light Stn.	44.350	-68.133	12	SAO	9/1/1974	Present	No
Great Duck Island Light Stn.	44.150	-68.250	0	SAO	9/1/1972	Present	No
Heron Neck Light Stn.	44.033	-68.867	0	SAO	10/1/1972	Present	No
Matinicus Rock	43.783	-68.850	16	SAO	3/1/1960	Present	No
Bar Harbor NAAS	44.450	-68.350	27	WBAN	7/1/1944	12/31/1945	No
Castine	44.383	-68.800	47	WBAN	1/1/1948	12/31/1950	No
Otter Point	44.317	-68.183	55	WBAN	7/1/1943	7/31/1944	No
Marsh-Billings-Rockefeller National Historical Park (MABI)							
Bethel	43.833	-72.633	165	COOP	11/20/1928	9/30/1957	No
Bethel 4 N	43.883	-72.635	201	COOP	5/1/1958	Present	No
Brownsville	43.500	-72.467	403	COOP	12/1/1968	2/28/1969	No
Cavendish	43.385	-72.599	257	COOP	2/17/1903	Present	No
Claremont Junction	43.367	-72.383	131	COOP	10/1/1897	5/1/1973	No
Cornish Flat	43.500	-72.283	259	COOP	5/1/1966	3/31/1985	No
Hanover	43.700	-72.283	184	COOP	11/1/1884	Present	No
Hanover 2	43.718	-72.272	162	COOP	10/1/1990	Present	No
Ludlow	43.394	-72.710	386	COOP	6/1/1970	5/1/2005	No
Ludlow 2	43.397	-72.688	296	COOP	10/1/1973	Present	No

Name	Lat.	Lon.	Elev. (m)	Network	Start	End	In Park?
Meriden	43.550	-72.267	296	COOP	6/1/1944	10/31/1957	No
Newport	43.383	-72.183	241	COOP	11/1/1928	Present	No
North Hartland Lake	43.603	-72.362	174	COOP	7/1/1961	Present	No
North Springfield	43.333	-72.517	146	COOP	11/1/1955	6/30/1956	No
North Springfield La	43.341	-72.507	171	COOP	5/1/1971	Present	No
Pittsfield	43.773	-72.815	259	COOP	6/1/1948	12/1/2002	No
Plymouth	43.533	-72.717	433	COOP	5/1/1941	3/31/1953	No
Plymouth Union	43.533	-72.733	372	COOP	11/1/1955	5/1/1970	No
Reading Hill	43.517	-72.567	451	COOP	6/1/1948	2/1/1968	No
Tyson	43.467	-72.700	336	COOP	6/1/1948	10/24/1973	No
Union Village Dam	43.797	-72.264	140	COOP	4/1/1950	Present	No
West Canaan	43.650	-72.100	214	COOP	5/1/1941	11/30/1955	No
West Hartford	43.717	-72.417	125	COOP	5/1/1930	10/31/1957	No
West Hartford 2	43.717	-72.417	114	COOP	4/1/1949	Present	No
West Lebanon	43.633	-72.317	116	COOP	12/1/1930	10/1/1969	No
West Windsor	43.467	-72.533	259	COOP	12/1/1969	4/7/1977	No
White River Junction	43.650	-72.317	110	COOP	11/1/1902	6/1/1985	No
Wilder	43.670	-72.308	111	COOP	1/1/1930	9/1/1998	No
Woodstock	43.622	-72.454	183	COOP	10/1/1892	Present	No
CW1064 Newport	43.400	-72.125	408	CWOP	M	Present	No
CW5240 Baltimore	43.346	-72.546	243	CWOP	M	Present	No
Lebanon Municipal AP	43.626	-72.305	181	SAO	7/1/1943	Present	No
Springfield Hartness State AP	43.344	-72.518	176	SAO	11/1/1970	Present	No
Lebanon AWO	43.533	-72.267	339	WBAN	7/7/1939	11/25/1940	No

Saint-Gaudens National Historic Site (SAGA)

Name	Lat.	Lon.	Elev. (m)	Network	Start	End	In Park?
Brownsville	43.500	-72.467	403	COOP	12/1/1968	2/28/1969	No
Cavendish	43.385	-72.599	257	COOP	2/17/1903	Present	No
Claremont Junction	43.367	-72.383	131	COOP	10/1/1897	5/1/1973	No
Cornish Flat	43.500	-72.283	259	COOP	5/1/1966	3/31/1985	No
Hanover	43.700	-72.283	184	COOP	11/1/1884	Present	No
Hanover 2	43.718	-72.272	162	COOP	10/1/1990	Present	No
Lebanon Municipal AP	43.626	-72.305	181	COOP	7/1/1943	Present	No
Ludlow	43.394	-72.710	386	COOP	6/1/1970	5/1/2005	No
Ludlow 2	43.397	-72.688	296	COOP	10/1/1973	Present	No
Meriden	43.550	-72.267	296	COOP	6/1/1944	10/31/1957	No
Mount Sunapee	43.333	-72.083	387	COOP	10/1/1957	Present	No
New London	43.417	-72.017	390	COOP	1/1/1947	9/1/1996	No
Newport	43.383	-72.183	241	COOP	11/1/1928	Present	No
North Hartland Lake	43.603	-72.362	174	COOP	7/1/1961	Present	No
North Springfield	43.333	-72.517	146	COOP	11/1/1955	6/30/1956	No
North Springfield La	43.341	-72.507	171	COOP	5/1/1971	Present	No
Pittsfield	43.773	-72.815	259	COOP	6/1/1948	12/1/2002	No
Plymouth	43.533	-72.717	433	COOP	5/1/1941	3/31/1953	No
Plymouth Union	43.533	-72.733	372	COOP	11/1/1955	5/1/1970	No
Reading Hill	43.517	-72.567	451	COOP	6/1/1948	2/1/1968	No

Name	Lat.	Lon.	Elev. (m)	Network	Start	End	In Park?
Springfield 2 SE	43.267	-72.450	92	COOP	10/7/1940	10/31/1958	No
Sunapee	43.383	-72.083	314	COOP	7/1/1941	11/20/1969	No
Tyson	43.467	-72.700	336	COOP	6/1/1948	10/24/1973	No
Union Village Dam	43.797	-72.264	140	COOP	4/1/1950	Present	No
Wendell	43.367	-72.117	287	COOP	6/1/1948	4/30/1954	No
West Canaan	43.650	-72.100	214	COOP	5/1/1941	11/30/1955	No
West Hartford	43.717	-72.417	125	COOP	5/1/1930	10/31/1957	No
West Hartford 2	43.717	-72.417	114	COOP	4/1/1949	Present	No
West Lebanon	43.633	-72.317	116	COOP	12/1/1930	10/1/1969	No
West Windsor	43.467	-72.533	259	COOP	12/1/1969	4/7/1977	No
White River Junction	43.650	-72.317	110	COOP	11/1/1902	6/1/1985	No
Wilder	43.670	-72.308	111	COOP	1/1/1930	9/1/1998	No
Woodstock	43.622	-72.454	183	COOP	10/1/1892	Present	No
CW1064 Newport	43.400	-72.125	408	CWOP	M	Present	No
CW5240 Baltimore	43.346	-72.546	243	CWOP	M	Present	No
CW5770 Charlestown	43.252	-72.413	147	CWOP	M	Present	No
N1ZGF New London	43.421	-72.010	390	CWOP	M	Present	No
Lebanon Municipal AP	43.626	-72.305	181	SAO	7/1/1943	Present	No
Springfield Hartness State AP	43.344	-72.518	176	SAO	11/1/1970	Present	No
Lebanon AWO	43.533	-72.267	339	WBAN	7/7/1939	11/25/1940	No
Saratoga National Historical Park (SARA)							
Sara	43.008	-73.651	114	RAWS	2/1/2003	Present	Yes
Albany County AP	42.743	-73.809	84	COOP	1/1/1874	Present	No
Battenville	43.101	-73.432	116	COOP	12/15/1952	Present	No
Cohoes	42.783	-73.717	15	COOP	3/1/1976	Present	No
Eagle Bridge 2 SE	42.933	-73.367	116	COOP	10/19/1951	Present	No
Fort Edward	43.267	-73.583	30	COOP	5/12/1987	Present	No
Glens Falls Fedr Dam	43.283	-73.667	92	COOP	5/1/1948	4/30/1956	No
Grafton	42.783	-73.467	475	COOP	8/1/1950	Present	No
Greenfield Center	43.117	-73.833	186	COOP	5/1/1903	7/31/1955	No
Johnsonville	42.917	-73.517	107	COOP	5/1/1948	6/30/1965	No
Mechanicville 2 S	42.883	-73.683	12	COOP	12/7/1903	3/31/1977	No
Melrose 1 NE	42.850	-73.617	107	COOP	7/1/1965	Present	No
Milton Center	43.050	-73.900	125	COOP	9/1/1987	2/1/1991	No
Round Lake 1 SE	42.924	-73.786	59	COOP	4/1/1992	Present	No
Salem	43.167	-73.317	149	COOP	9/1/1942	3/1/1998	No
Saratoga Springs 4 N	43.100	-73.833	168	COOP	2/1/1895	11/30/1951	No
Saratoga Springs 4 S	43.033	-73.817	94	COOP	7/1/1955	Present	No
Schaghticoke 1 W	42.900	-73.600	40	COOP	5/1/1948	6/30/1965	No
Schenectady	42.800	-73.917	110	COOP	7/1/1988	1/1/1997	No
Schenectady	42.833	-73.917	67	COOP	11/1/1898	9/1/1985	No
Schenectady Solar Ra	42.833	-73.883	149	COOP	7/1/1952	Present	No
Schuylerville	43.113	-73.578	37	COOP	5/1/1948	Present	No
Schuylerville Lock 5	43.117	-73.583	34	COOP	1/1/1932	8/31/1963	No
Spier Falls	43.233	-73.750	119	COOP	8/1/1901	10/1/1975	No

Name	Lat.	Lon.	Elev. (m)	Network	Start	End	In Park?
Troy L & D	42.750	-73.683	7	COOP	11/1/1932	Present	No
West Milton	43.033	-73.933	134	COOP	10/1/1955	1/1/1986	No
CW0300 Spigletown	42.805	-73.608	195	CWOP	M	Present	No
CW0508 Troy	42.745	-73.684	12	CWOP	M	Present	No
CW1411 Vischer Ferry	42.795	-73.823	66	CWOP	M	Present	No
CW1762 Scotia	42.848	-73.967	85	CWOP	M	Present	No
CW2496 Schenectady	42.817	-73.912	110	CWOP	M	Present	No
CW3343 Niskayuna	42.832	-73.880	104	CWOP	M	Present	No
CW3586 Hoosick Falls	42.870	-73.408	305	CWOP	M	Present	No
CW3692 Glens Falls	43.273	-73.657	106	CWOP	M	Present	No
CW3725 Vischer Ferry	42.795	-73.823	65	CWOP	M	Present	No
CW4574 Galway	43.000	-74.000	229	CWOP	M	Present	No
CW5184 Clifton Park	42.817	-73.785	89	CWOP	M	Present	No
W2GWY Glen Falls	43.284	-73.654	107	CWOP	M	Present	No
Hudson Falls	43.270	-73.540	72	GPS-MET	M	Present	No
Albany County AP	42.743	-73.809	84	SAO	1/1/1874	Present	No
Schenectady	42.850	-73.950	101	SAO	4/1/1948	Present	No
Ballston Spa	42.973	-73.839	71	WX4U	M	Present	No
Saratoga Springs	43.000	-73.730	100	WX4U	M	Present	No

As previously mentioned, SARA has one station located within its park boundaries (Table 4.3; Figure 4.1). This is a RAWS station (Sara) which is currently active, is automated, and has operated since 2003. The best source for long-term climate records come from the stations at the Albany International Airport, almost 30 km southwest of SARA. Stations have operated here since 1874 and include a COOP station and a SAO station (both are named "Albany County AP" in this report). The data records from these two stations are complete with no significant data gaps. Another source of long-term climate data is the COOP station "Troy L & D," which has operated since 1932. This station is also about 30 km southwest of SARA. The most notable data gaps are present in July during the late 1990s and in June 2005. Other than these gaps, the data record at "Troy L & D" is quite complete. Several other COOP stations provide data records that go back to the late 1940s and the 1950s. The closest of these to SARA is the COOP station "Schuylerville," about 10 km north of SARA along the Hudson River. Besides the SAO station "Albany County AP," an SAO station at Schenectady currently provides near-real-time observations about 25 km southwest of SARA. This station has been active since 1948. At least 12 CWOP station also provide near-real-time weather data within 30 km of SARA.

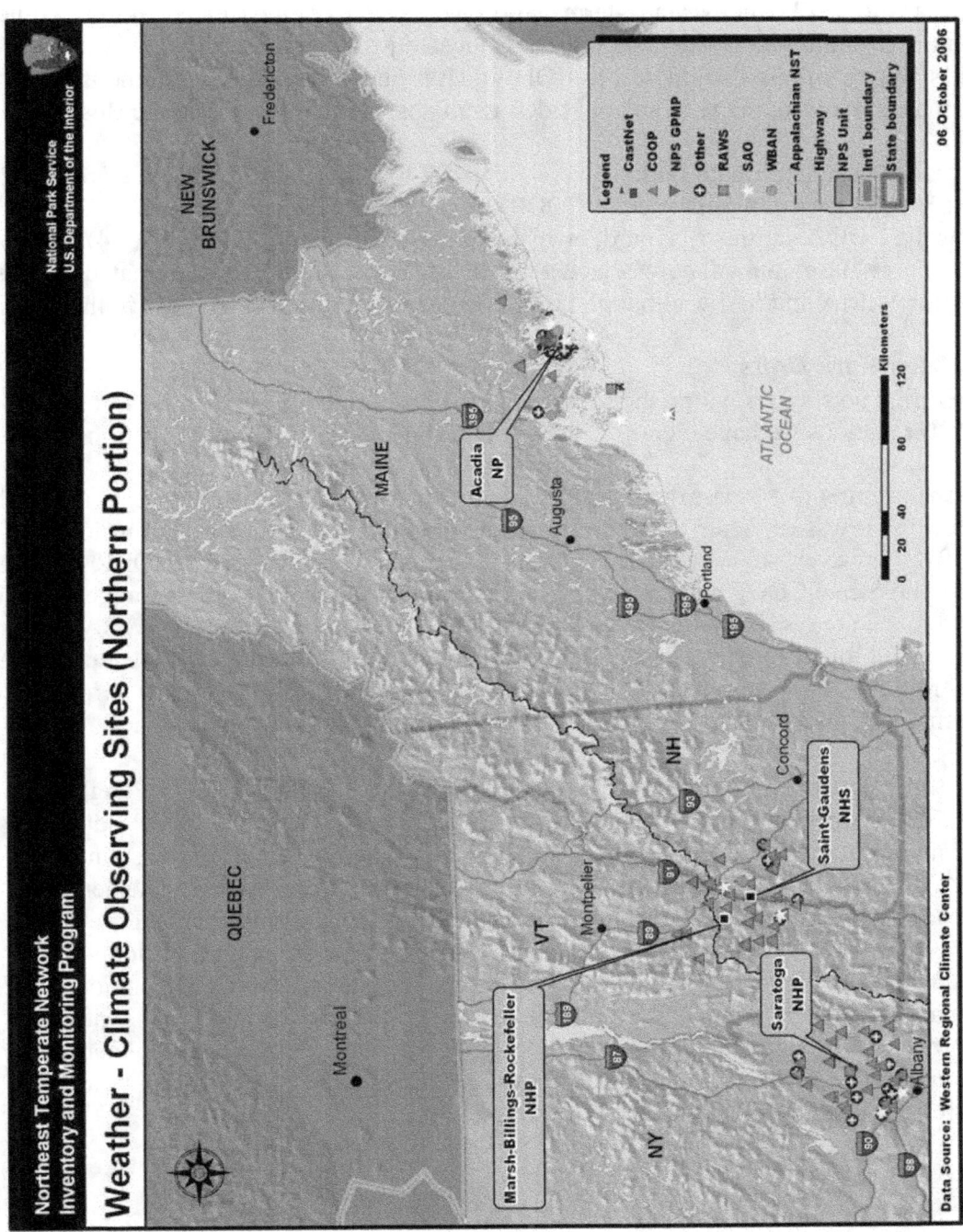

Figure 4.1. Station locations for the northern NETN park units.

4.2.2. Boston Area Park Units

No stations have been identified within BOHA (Figure 4.2; Table 4.4). There are 47 stations we have identified within 10 km of BOHA, with 33 of these being active. Four of the active stations are COOP stations. The records at each of these stations go back at least several decades. The shortest record is from 1960 at the COOP station "Hingham." The data record from this site is very complete, with almost no data gaps. Boston's Logan International Airport has provided reliable observations since 1920 at the COOP station "Boston Logan Intl. Arpt.," just west of BOHA. The longest data record, however, is at "Boston City WSO," which has a reliable data record going back to 1872. Another long-term station worth noting is the COOP station at Blue Hill Observatory in southwest Boston, although it is located just over 10 km southwest of BOHA. This station is of possible interest to BOHA as it is one of the oldest continuously-operating climate stations in the U.S. and provides a valuable climate record for the Boston area.

Many of the same weather/climate stations were identified for MIMA and SAIR as were identified for BOHA. One additional active COOP station was identified for both MIMA and SAIR. This is the COOP station "Maynard," which has operated since 1974 (Table 4.4). Hanscom Air Force Base, immediately adjacent to MIMA, may also provide automated weather observations for MIMA and SAIR, although no stations were identified at the base in this report.

4.2.3. Southern Park Units

We have identified no stations within the southern park units of the NETN (Figure 4.3; Table 4.5). Most of the stations we have identified are either COOP stations or CWOP stations.

Due to the urban setting of Morristown National Historical Park (MORR) in the western suburbs of New York City, it was expected that there would be many weather/climate stations located close to MORR. However, we have only identified 11 stations within 10 km of MORR (Table 4.5). There are no active COOP stations within this distance of MORR. The best source for near-real-time data in the area is likely from Morristown Municipal Airport (listed as a WBAN station in Table 4.5), about four kilometers east of MORR. Other sources for near-real-time data in the area may be from the SAO stations located over 30 km east of MORR at Teterboro Airport, Newark International Airport, and the international airports around New York City.

The primary source of near-real-time weather data for ROVA is the SAO station "Poughkeepsie Dutchess Co. AP," which has been in operation since 1932 (Table 4.5). Ten CWOP stations also provide automated data within 30 km of ROVA. There are 13 active COOP stations within 30 km of ROVA. The closest COOP stations are at least 10 km away from ROVA. The densest coverage of stations is just over 10 km south of ROVA along the Hudson River (Figure 4.3). Besides the COOP and SAO stations at Poughkeepsie's Dutchess County Airport, long-term climate data are also available from a few COOP stations in the area. Two COOP stations, "Mohonk Lake" and "Wappingers Falls," provide data going back to the late 1800s. Although the data record at "Wappingers Falls" goes back to 1893, the data quality and completeness for the station could not be verified in this report. On the other hand, the COOP station "Mohonk Lake" has a reliable data record going back to 1896.

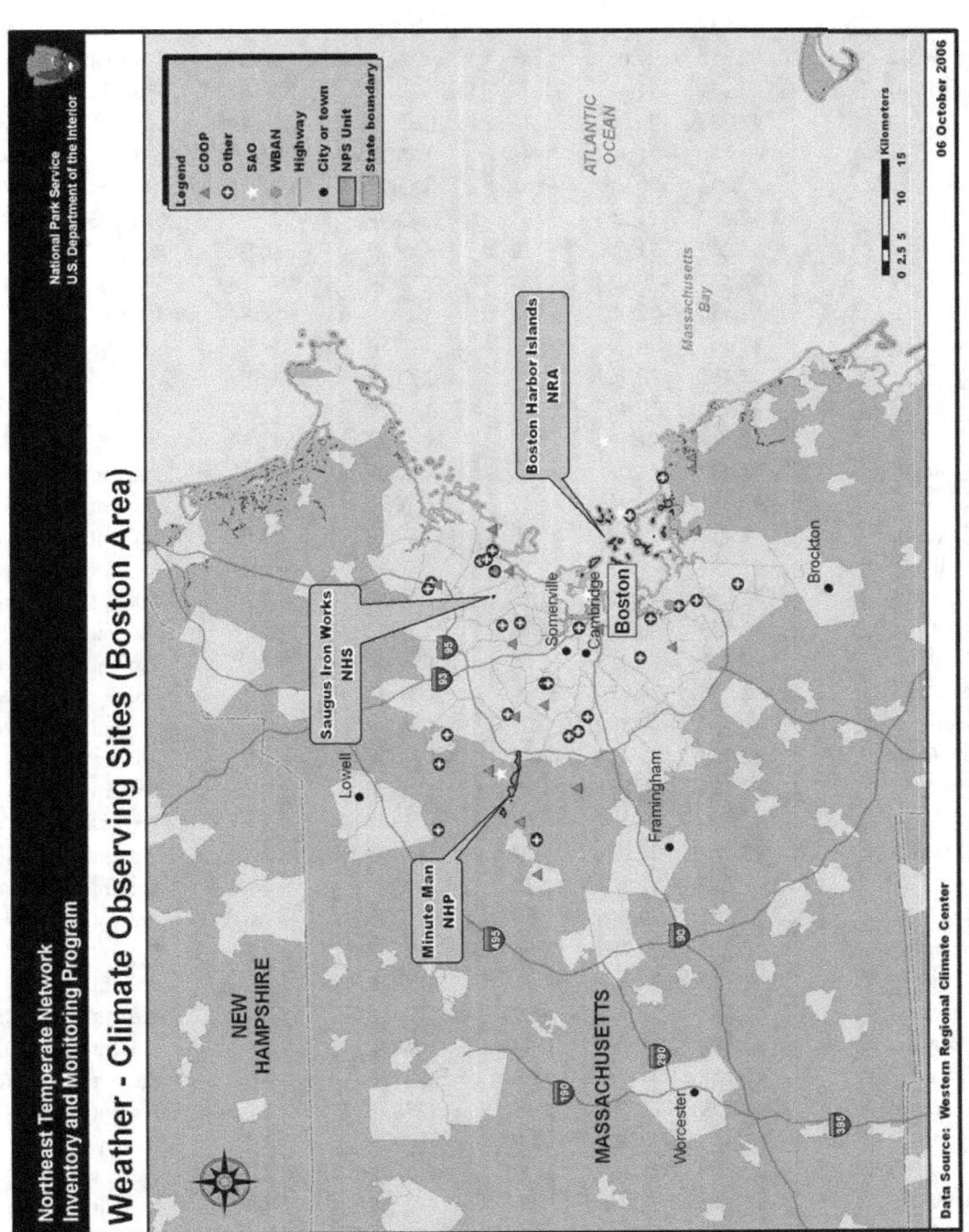

Figure 4.2. Station locations for the NETN park units in and near Boston, Massachusetts.

35

Table 4.4. Weather/climate stations for the NETN park units in and near Boston, Massachusetts. Stations inside park units and within 10 km of the park unit boundary are included. Missing entries are indicated by "M".

Name	Lat.	Lon.	Elev. (m)	Network	Start	End	In Park?
Boston Harbor Islands National Recreation Area (BOHA)							
Arlington	42.417	-71.183	55	COOP	1/1/1943	7/31/1950	No
Bedford	42.483	-71.283	49	COOP	5/1/1957	Present	No
Beechwood	42.233	-70.817	19	COOP	2/1/1936	4/1/1996	No
Boston City WSO	42.350	-71.067	6	COOP	1/1/1872	Present	No
Boston Logan Intl. Arpt.	42.361	-71.011	6	COOP	1/1/1920	Present	No
Cohasset	42.233	-70.800	15	COOP	7/1/1895	9/30/1960	No
Concord	42.450	-71.367	43	COOP	1/1/1893	1/31/1950	No
Hingham	42.233	-70.917	9	COOP	9/1/1960	Present	No
Lexington	42.450	-71.200	61	COOP	3/1/1951	8/31/1956	No
Mattapan	42.267	-71.100	12	COOP	11/1/1958	7/1/2002	No
Peabody	42.533	-70.983	52	COOP	9/1/1965	3/1/1995	No
Spot Pond	42.450	-71.083	52	COOP	6/1/1904	8/1/1977	No
Swampscott	42.467	-70.900	6	COOP	1/1/1929	3/31/1957	No
West Lynn	42.467	-70.967	37	COOP	3/1/1957	9/30/1959	No
West Lynn Solar Rad	42.450	-70.967	24	COOP	7/1/1952	8/31/1952	No
Weston	42.383	-71.317	67	COOP	8/1/1896	7/1/1968	No
CW0210 Malden	42.439	-71.051	16	CWOP	M	Present	No
CW0934 Lynn	42.481	-70.949	17	CWOP	M	Present	No
CW0983 Concord	42.431	-71.396	20	CWOP	M	Present	No
CW1017 Arlington	42.414	-71.150	14	CWOP	M	Present	No
CW1097 Billerica	42.540	-71.270	107	CWOP	M	Present	No
CW1374 Peabody	42.543	-70.990	10	CWOP	M	Present	No
CW1378 Boston	42.235	-71.028	40	CWOP	M	Present	No
CW2330 Milton	42.256	-71.036	5	CWOP	M	Present	No
CW2404 Hull	42.307	-70.889	25	CWOP	M	Present	No
CW3246 Waltham	42.389	-71.235	70	CWOP	M	Present	No
CW3803 Hull	42.267	-70.831	10	CWOP	M	Present	No
CW3832 Melrose	42.460	-71.054	32	CWOP	M	Present	No
CW3925 Billerica	42.529	-71.224	57	CWOP	M	Present	No
CW4655 Waltham	42.378	-71.228	15	CWOP	M	Present	No
CW5601 Lynn	42.474	-70.946	23	CWOP	M	Present	No
K1EMS Peabody	42.539	-70.980	50	CWOP	M	Present	No
K1LCQ Boston	42.289	-71.054	11	CWOP	M	Present	No
K3NA Charlestown	42.372	-71.063	29	CWOP	M	Present	No
KA1TOX Braintree	42.187	-71.005	40	CWOP	M	Present	No
KB1JKP Concord	42.431	-71.395	59	CWOP	M	Present	No
N1EPX Jamaica Plain	42.303	-71.116	15	CWOP	M	Present	No
N1EVH Lynn	42.465	-70.966	8	CWOP	M	Present	No
N1JDU-3 Watertown	42.367	-71.206	5	CWOP	M	Present	No
N1OTX Woburn	42.458	-71.196	49	CWOP	M	Present	No
Bedford Hanscom Field	42.470	-71.289	41	SAO	9/1/1942	Present	No

Name	Lat.	Lon.	Elev. (m)	Network	Start	End	In Park?
Boston Light Stn.	42.317	-70.883	0	SAO	4/23/1975	Present	No
Boston Lightship	42.333	-70.767	6	SAO	9/16/1927	5/2/1975	No
Boston Logan Intl. Arpt.	42.361	-71.011	6	SAO	1/1/1920	Present	No
Squantum NAS	42.267	-71.033	5	WBAN	3/1/1942	12/31/1953	No
Arlington Center Arlington	42.410	-71.150	14	WX4U	M	Present	No
Lynn	42.467	-70.933	5	WX4U	M	Present	No
Minute Man National Historical Park (MIMA)							
Arlington	42.417	-71.183	55	COOP	1/1/1943	7/31/1950	No
Bedford	42.483	-71.283	49	COOP	5/1/1957	Present	No
Boston City WSO	42.350	-71.067	6	COOP	1/1/1872	Present	No
Boston Logan Intl. Arpt.	42.361	-71.011	6	COOP	1/1/1920	Present	No
Concord	42.450	-71.367	43	COOP	1/1/1893	1/31/1950	No
Hingham	42.233	-70.917	9	COOP	9/1/1960	Present	No
Lexington	42.450	-71.200	61	COOP	3/1/1951	8/31/1956	No
Mattapan	42.267	-71.100	12	COOP	11/1/1958	7/1/2002	No
Maynard	42.433	-71.450	66	COOP	5/1/1974	Present	No
Peabody	42.533	-70.983	52	COOP	9/1/1965	3/1/1995	No
Spot Pond	42.450	-71.083	52	COOP	6/1/1904	8/1/1977	No
Swampscott	42.467	-70.900	6	COOP	1/1/1929	3/31/1957	No
West Lynn	42.467	-70.967	37	COOP	3/1/1957	9/30/1959	No
West Lynn Solar Rad	42.450	-70.967	24	COOP	7/1/1952	8/31/1952	No
Weston	42.383	-71.317	67	COOP	8/1/1896	7/1/1968	No
CW0003 Carlisle	42.544	-71.374	61	CWOP	M	Present	No
CW0210 Malden	42.439	-71.051	16	CWOP	M	Present	No
CW0934 Lynn	42.481	-70.949	17	CWOP	M	Present	No
CW0983 Concord	42.431	-71.396	20	CWOP	M	Present	No
CW1017 Arlington	42.414	-71.150	14	CWOP	M	Present	No
CW1097 Billerica	42.540	-71.270	107	CWOP	M	Present	No
CW1374 Peabody	42.543	-70.990	10	CWOP	M	Present	No
CW1378 Boston	42.235	-71.028	40	CWOP	M	Present	No
CW2330 Milton	42.256	-71.036	5	CWOP	M	Present	No
CW2404 Hull	42.307	-70.889	25	CWOP	M	Present	No
CW3246 Waltham	42.389	-71.235	70	CWOP	M	Present	No
CW3832 Melrose	42.460	-71.054	32	CWOP	M	Present	No
CW3925 Billerica	42.529	-71.224	57	CWOP	M	Present	No
CW4655 Waltham	42.378	-71.228	15	CWOP	M	Present	No
CW5601 Lynn	42.474	-70.946	23	CWOP	M	Present	No
K1EMS Peabody	42.539	-70.980	50	CWOP	M	Present	No
K1LCQ Boston	42.289	-71.054	11	CWOP	M	Present	No
K3NA Charlestown	42.372	-71.063	29	CWOP	M	Present	No
KA1TOX Braintree	42.187	-71.005	40	CWOP	M	Present	No
KB1JKP Concord	42.431	-71.395	59	CWOP	M	Present	No
N1EPX Jamaica Plain	42.303	-71.116	15	CWOP	M	Present	No
N1EVH Lynn	42.465	-70.966	8	CWOP	M	Present	No
N1JDU-3 Watertown	42.367	-71.206	5	CWOP	M	Present	No
N1OTX Woburn	42.458	-71.196	49	CWOP	M	Present	No

Name	Lat.	Lon.	Elev. (m)	Network	Start	End	In Park?
Bedford Hanscom Field	42.470	-71.289	41	SAO	9/1/1942	Present	No
Boston Light Stn.	42.317	-70.883	0	SAO	4/23/1975	Present	No
Boston Logan Intl. Arpt.	42.361	-71.011	6	SAO	1/1/1920	Present	No
Squantum NAS	42.267	-71.033	5	WBAN	3/1/1942	12/31/1953	No
Arlington Center Arlington	42.410	-71.150	14	WX4U	M	Present	No
Lynn	42.467	-70.933	5	WX4U	M	Present	No

Saugus Iron Works National Historic Site (SAIR)

Name	Lat.	Lon.	Elev. (m)	Network	Start	End	In Park?
Arlington	42.417	-71.183	55	COOP	1/1/1943	7/31/1950	No
Bedford	42.483	-71.283	49	COOP	5/1/1957	Present	No
Beechwood	42.233	-70.817	19	COOP	2/1/1936	4/1/1996	No
Boston City WSO	42.350	-71.067	6	COOP	1/1/1872	Present	No
Boston Logan Intl. Arpt.	42.361	-71.011	6	COOP	1/1/1920	Present	No
Cohasset	42.233	-70.800	15	COOP	7/1/1895	9/30/1960	No
Concord	42.450	-71.367	43	COOP	1/1/1893	1/31/1950	No
Hingham	42.233	-70.917	9	COOP	9/1/1960	Present	No
Lexington	42.450	-71.200	61	COOP	3/1/1951	8/31/1956	No
Mattapan	42.267	-71.100	12	COOP	11/1/1958	7/1/2002	No
Maynard	42.433	-71.450	66	COOP	5/1/1974	Present	No
Peabody	42.533	-70.983	52	COOP	9/1/1965	3/1/1995	No
Spot Pond	42.450	-71.083	52	COOP	6/1/1904	8/1/1977	No
Swampscott	42.467	-70.900	6	COOP	1/1/1929	3/31/1957	No
West Lynn	42.467	-70.967	37	COOP	3/1/1957	9/30/1959	No
West Lynn Solar Rad	42.450	-70.967	24	COOP	7/1/1952	8/31/1952	No
Weston	42.383	-71.317	67	COOP	8/1/1896	7/1/1968	No
CW0003 Carlisle	42.544	-71.374	61	CWOP	M	Present	No
CW0210 Malden	42.439	-71.051	16	CWOP	M	Present	No
CW0934 Lynn	42.481	-70.949	17	CWOP	M	Present	No
CW0983 Concord	42.431	-71.396	20	CWOP	M	Present	No
CW1017 Arlington	42.414	-71.150	14	CWOP	M	Present	No
CW1097 Billerica	42.540	-71.270	107	CWOP	M	Present	No
CW1374 Peabody	42.543	-70.990	10	CWOP	M	Present	No
CW1378 Boston	42.235	-71.028	40	CWOP	M	Present	No
CW2330 Milton	42.256	-71.036	5	CWOP	M	Present	No
CW2404 Hull	42.307	-70.889	25	CWOP	M	Present	No
CW3246 Waltham	42.389	-71.235	70	CWOP	M	Present	No
CW3803 Hull	42.267	-70.831	10	CWOP	M	Present	No
CW3832 Melrose	42.460	-71.054	32	CWOP	M	Present	No
CW3925 Billerica	42.529	-71.224	57	CWOP	M	Present	No
CW4655 Waltham	42.378	-71.228	15	CWOP	M	Present	No
CW5601 Lynn	42.474	-70.946	23	CWOP	M	Present	No
K1EMS Peabody	42.539	-70.980	50	CWOP	M	Present	No
K1LCQ Boston	42.289	-71.054	11	CWOP	M	Present	No
K3NA Charlestown	42.372	-71.063	29	CWOP	M	Present	No
KA1TOX Braintree	42.187	-71.005	40	CWOP	M	Present	No
KB1JKP Concord	42.431	-71.395	59	CWOP	M	Present	No
N1EPX Jamaica Plain	42.303	-71.116	15	CWOP	M	Present	No

Name	Lat.	Lon.	Elev. (m)	Network	Start	End	In Park?
N1EVH Lynn	42.465	-70.966	8	CWOP	M	Present	No
N1JDU-3 Watertown	42.367	-71.206	5	CWOP	M	Present	No
N1OTX Woburn	42.458	-71.196	49	CWOP	M	Present	No
Bedford Hanscom Field	42.470	-71.289	41	SAO	9/1/1942	Present	No
Boston Light Stn.	42.317	-70.883	0	SAO	4/23/1975	Present	No
Boston Lightship	42.333	-70.767	6	SAO	9/16/1927	5/2/1975	No
Boston Logan Intl. Arpt.	42.361	-71.011	6	SAO	1/1/1920	Present	No
Squantum NAS	42.267	-71.033	5	WBAN	3/1/1942	12/31/1953	No
Arlington Center Arlington	42.410	-71.150	14	WX4U	M	Present	No
Lynn	42.467	-70.933	5	WX4U	M	Present	No

Eleven COOP stations are currently active within 30 km of WEFA. Of these, the longest data record comes from the COOP station "Stevenson Dam," which has been operating since 1893 (Table 4.5). However, this station has unreliable data. The next longest data record is from the COOP station "Danbury" (1937-present), about 15 km north of WEFA (Figure 4.3). A significant data gap occurred at this station from September 1986 to January 1990. Outside of this gap, the data record at "Danbury" is complete. The COOP and SAO stations at Bridgeport's Sikorsky Memorial Airport are reliable sources of climate data and are located about 20 km east of WEFA. Other near-real-time data sources are the SAO sites at Danbury Municipal Airport, 15 km north of WEFA, and Westchester County Airport, almost 30 km southwest of WEFA.

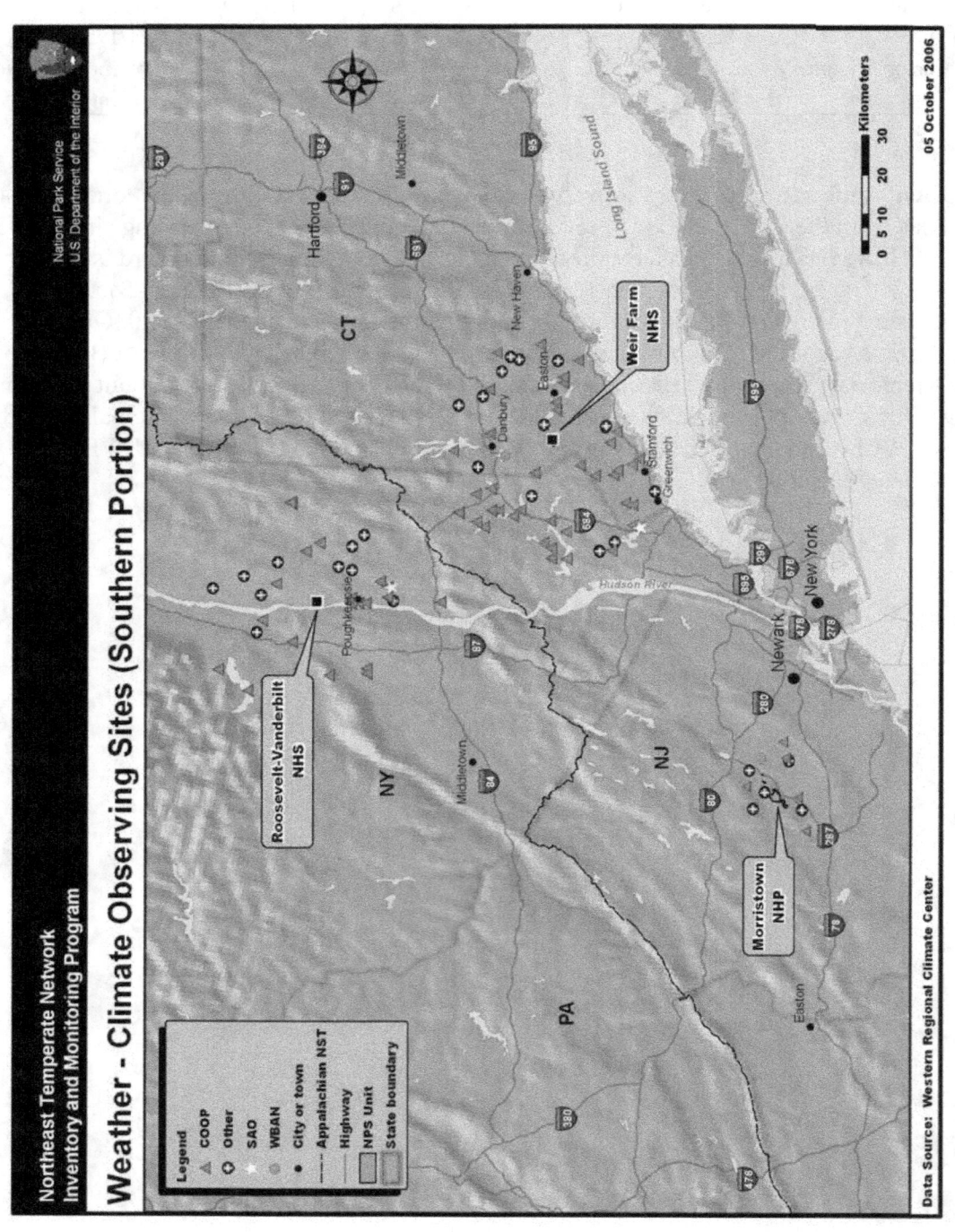

Figure 4.3. Station locations for the southern NETN park units.

40

Table 4.5. Weather/climate stations for the southern NETN park units. Stations inside MORR and within 10 km of MORR are indicated. Stations inside park units and within 30 km of the park unit boundary are indicated for ROVA and WEFA. Missing entries are indicated by "M".

Name	Lat.	Lon.	Elev. (m)	Network	Start	End	In Park?
Morristown National Historical Park (MORR)							
Bernardsville 2 E	40.717	-74.533	73	COOP	4/1/1959	3/31/1979	No
Chatham	40.750	-74.367	58	COOP	2/17/1903	11/19/1965	No
Chatham 2 W	40.744	-74.416	108	COOP	4/1/2000	2/1/2004	No
Far Hills 2 N	40.700	-74.633	68	COOP	11/1/1979	1/15/2004	No
Morris Plains 1 W	40.833	-74.500	122	COOP	7/1/1941	1/1/1992	No
CW0154 Cedar Knolls	40.826	-74.454	104	CWOP	M	Present	No
CW1931 Morristown	40.792	-74.519	111	CWOP	M	Present	No
CW2914 Bernardsville	40.708	-74.572	133	CWOP	M	Present	No
KC2ENI Randolph	40.818	-74.569	253	CWOP	M	Present	No
KC2RLM-1 Chatham	40.737	-74.425	80	CWOP	M	Present	No
Morristown Muni. Arpt.	40.800	-74.417	57	WBAN	3/1/1962	Present	No
Roosevelt-Vanderbilt National Historical Park (ROVA)							
Carmel 4 N	41.473	-73.655	207	COOP	12/13/2001	Present	No
Clinton Corners	41.817	-73.767	85	COOP	8/1/1971	Present	No
Gardiner 1 W	41.683	-74.150	98	COOP	12/1/1956	Present	No
Glenford	42.017	-74.133	262	COOP	5/1/1948	11/30/1974	No
Glenham	41.517	-73.933	84	COOP	2/1/1932	10/1/1996	No
High Falls	41.833	-74.133	43	COOP	1/1/1927	10/1/1967	No
Kingston City Hall	41.917	-73.983	15	COOP	5/1/1948	3/21/1984	No
Kingston Gas Plant	41.917	-73.983	3	COOP	8/1/1957	6/30/1959	No
Millbrook	41.850	-73.617	250	COOP	11/20/1941	Present	No
Millbrook 3 W	41.786	-73.742	134	COOP	11/1/2004	Present	No
Mohonk Lake	41.768	-74.155	379	COOP	1/1/1896	Present	No
New Hackensack	41.633	-73.883	46	COOP	9/1/1939	10/31/1948	No
New Paltz 4 SW	41.683	-74.133	128	COOP	1/1/1972	4/1/1983	No
Poughkeepsie	41.633	-73.917	52	COOP	11/15/1993	Present	No
Poughkeepsie	41.683	-73.933	31	COOP	1/1/1893	10/31/1974	No
Poughkeepsie 1 N	41.717	-73.933	15	COOP	6/1/1962	Present	No
Poughkeepsie Dutchess Co. AP	41.627	-73.884	51	COOP	12/1/1932	Present	No
Poughkeepsie Midtown	41.700	-73.933	3	COOP	2/1/1960	11/30/1974	No
Poughkeepsie Pendell	41.717	-73.917	67	COOP	4/1/1965	7/31/1976	No
Rhinebeck 4 SE	41.885	-73.869	92	COOP	10/12/1989	Present	No
Rifton 1 N	41.850	-74.050	12	COOP	10/1/1921	10/1/1967	No
Rosendale 2 E	41.850	-74.050	12	COOP	11/1/1956	Present	No
Shokan Brown Station	41.950	-74.200	155	COOP	5/1/1940	Present	No
Wappingers Falls	41.650	-73.867	35	COOP	3/1/1893	Present	No
CW0484 Rhinebeck	41.956	-73.844	107	CWOP	M	Present	No
CW2434 Lagrangeville	41.684	-73.720	202	CWOP	M	Present	No
CW2607 Rhinebeck	41.918	-73.905	70	CWOP	M	Present	No
CW2673 Pleasant Valley	41.743	-73.817	100	CWOP	M	Present	No

Name	Lat.	Lon.	Elev. (m)	Network	Start	End	In Park?
CW3054 LaGrange	41.713	-73.829	134	CWOP	M	Present	No
CW3362 Schultzville	41.879	-73.801	143	CWOP	M	Present	No
CW4484 Lagrange	41.712	-73.754	123	CWOP	M	Present	No
N2EYH Wappingers Falls	41.620	-73.929	58	CWOP	M	Present	No
N3EYQ Kingston	41.928	-74.020	58	CWOP	M	Present	No
W2DAV Red Hook	42.025	-73.883	75	CWOP	M	Present	No
Poughkeepsie Dutchess Co. AP	41.627	-73.884	51	SAO	12/1/1932	Present	No

Weir Farm National Historic Site (WEFA)

Name	Lat.	Lon.	Elev. (m)	Network	Start	End	In Park?
Amawalk	41.283	-73.750	116	COOP	5/1/1948	11/30/1974	No
Bedford Hills	41.233	-73.717	131	COOP	7/1/1899	6/1/1977	No
Brewster	41.433	-73.600	189	COOP	5/1/1948	10/31/1948	No
Bridgeport	41.200	-73.200	43	COOP	8/20/1893	3/31/1951	No
Bridgeport Sikorsky Memorial A	41.158	-73.129	2	COOP	12/1/1941	Present	No
Candlewood Lake	41.483	-73.467	153	COOP	6/1/1948	4/30/1975	No
Carmel	41.433	-73.683	162	COOP	1/1/1888	3/1/1996	No
Carmel 4 N	41.473	-73.655	207	COOP	12/13/2001	Present	No
Cross River	41.267	-73.683	73	COOP	5/1/1948	11/30/1974	No
Croton Falls 1 NE	41.350	-73.667	67	COOP	5/1/1948	11/30/1974	No
Croton Lake	41.233	-73.800	76	COOP	5/1/1948	11/30/1974	No
Danbury	41.400	-73.417	123	COOP	10/1/1937	Present	No
East Branch	41.400	-73.583	140	COOP	5/1/1948	11/30/1974	No
Easton Reservoir	41.233	-73.250	52	COOP	6/1/1948	10/31/1975	No
Glenbrook	41.083	-73.517	15	COOP	3/1/1958	3/2/1959	No
Greenwich	41.083	-73.700	137	COOP	11/12/1947	12/31/1953	No
Hemlocks Reservoir	41.233	-73.267	73	COOP	6/1/1948	4/30/1974	No
Laurel Reservoir	41.167	-73.550	107	COOP	6/1/1948	4/30/1974	No
Mead Pond Reservoir	41.200	-73.517	146	COOP	6/1/1948	4/30/1974	No
Middle Branch Reservoir	41.383	-73.650	116	COOP	5/1/1948	11/30/1974	No
Newtown	41.400	-73.283	137	COOP	10/1/1957	Present	No
North Stamford Reservoir	41.117	-73.533	61	COOP	6/1/1948	6/30/1950	No
Norwalk	41.133	-73.450	37	COOP	1/1/1893	4/30/1956	No
Norwalk Gas Plant	41.117	-73.417	11	COOP	4/1/1956	1/1/1988	No
Pleasantville	41.131	-73.776	98	COOP	5/8/1944	11/9/2000	No
Putnam Lake	41.083	-73.639	91	COOP	6/1/1948	Present	No
Rockwood Lake	41.100	-73.633	101	COOP	6/1/1948	12/31/1950	No
Round Pond	41.301	-73.537	244	COOP	6/1/1948	Present	No
Saugatuck Reservoir	41.250	-73.350	91	COOP	6/1/1948	Present	No
Stamford 2nd Order	41.067	-73.500	34	COOP	7/1/1950	9/30/1955	No
Stamford 5 N	41.125	-73.548	58	COOP	9/1/1955	Present	No
Stevenson Dam	41.382	-73.172	35	COOP	1/1/1893	Present	No
Tilly Foster	41.400	-73.650	122	COOP	11/1/1948	12/31/1953	No
Titicus	41.333	-73.650	82	COOP	5/1/1948	11/30/1974	No
Trap Falls Reservoir	41.283	-73.150	98	COOP	6/1/1948	10/31/1975	No
West Branch	41.417	-73.700	153	COOP	5/1/1948	9/30/1952	No

Name	Lat.	Lon.	Elev. (m)	Network	Start	End	In Park?
White Plains Westchester Co. AP	41.067	-73.708	116	COOP	4/1/1946	Present	No
Yorktown Heights	41.267	-73.767	128	COOP	1/1/1942	1/31/1950	No
Yorktown Heights 1 W	41.266	-73.798	204	COOP	4/1/1965	Present	No
CW0179 Norwalk	41.141	-73.403	31	CWOP	M	Present	No
CW2608 Monroe	41.331	-73.195	168	CWOP	M	Present	No
CW3288 Newtown	41.414	-73.304	137	CWOP	M	Present	No
CW4284 Pleasantville	41.124	-73.751	137	CWOP	M	Present	No
CW5055 Trumbull	41.243	-73.201	76	CWOP	M	Present	No
CW5606 Danbury	41.428	-73.517	277	CWOP	M	Present	No
CW5640 Newtown	41.468	-73.330	86	CWOP	M	Present	No
K2LCA Chappaqua	41.158	-73.778	147	CWOP	M	Present	No
K2LCA-1 Chappaqua	41.159	-73.777	107	CWOP	M	Present	No
K6SEM-15 Waccabuc	41.308	-73.608	150	CWOP	M	Present	No
KB8TQ-13 Redding	41.278	-73.392	145	CWOP	M	Present	No
W1CWS-1 Cos Cob	41.032	-73.600	18	CWOP	M	Present	No
Bridgeport Sikorsky Memorial A	41.158	-73.129	2	SAO	12/1/1941	Present	No
Danbury Municipal AP	41.371	-73.483	139	SAO	5/1/1973	Present	No
White Plains Westchester Co. AP	41.067	-73.708	116	SAO	4/1/1946	Present	No
Danbury	41.367	-73.483	61	WBAN	M	Present	No
Stamford 2nd Order	41.050	-73.533	0	WBAN	3/1/1934	12/31/1937	No
Stratford	41.167	-73.133	4	WBAN	12/1/1942	6/30/1944	No
Barn Hill Monroe	41.349	-73.185	193	WX4U	M	Present	No
New Milford	41.370	-73.230	164	WX4U	M	Present	No
Stonybrook Norwalk	41.140	-73.400	26	WX4U	M	Present	No

5.0. Conclusions and Recommendations

We have based our findings on an examination of the available records and the topography and climate within NETN units, discussions with NPS staff and other collaborators, and prior knowledge of the area. Here, we offer an evaluation and general comments pertaining to the status, prospects, and needs for climate-monitoring capabilities in NETN.

5.1. Northeast Temperate Inventory and Monitoring Network

Besides SARA, ACAD is the only park unit with weather/climate stations located within its boundaries. This helps to illustrate how important it is for NETN park units to rely on outside sources of weather and climate data. Most of the NETN park units have a relatively dense coverage of nearby weather/climate stations. This is true especially for the park units near Boston and New York City. Most of these park units have several nearby COOP stations that have lengthy periods of record. Near-real-time observations are generally available from SAO station located at major airports, especially in the Boston and New York City regions. The one exception to this general pattern appears to be MORR, which despite its location within the suburbs west of New York City, has no active COOP stations or SAO stations within 10 km of the park unit. The only sources for near-real-time data we have identified for MORR are five CWOP stations within 10 km of the park unit. The best sources for near-real-time data may therefore be from the SAO stations at Newark International Airport and the international airports in New York City. All of these are at least 30 km east of MORR.

Since the COOP station "Acadia National Park" is the only COOP station within 30 km of ACAD that has a data record longer than two decades, it is essential that NPS actively work with the NWS offices in this region to help ensure that this valuable station remains active and provides useful data for NPS research and management activities. The closest NWS office for ACAD would be the forecast office at Portland, Maine (http://www.erh.noaa.gov/gyx). The only source of automated weather data we identified inside ACAD is the GPMP station on Cadillac Mountain. For weather conditions at sea level, ACAD must utilize observations from the SAO stations at Bar Harbor Airport and the various light stations along the coast near ACAD. The SAO station at Bar Harbor Airport is also the best source for long-term climate records for ACAD.

5.2. Spatial Variations in Mean Climate

Land cover is a major controlling factor of local- and regional-scale spatial variations in mean surface climate within NETN. With local variations over short horizontal and vertical distances, variations in land cover introduce considerable fine-scale structure to mean climate, (temperature and precipitation). Topography and proximity to the Atlantic Ocean are also controlling factors for spatial climate patterns in NETN park units, influencing certain aspects of climate such as spatial variations in temperature during stable weather conditions in the winter months (temperature inversions, cold-air drainages, etc.). Issues encountered in mapping mean spatial patterns of climate are discussed further in Appendix E.

For areas in which there are already numerous weather/climate stations, much of this spatial variability can be described by the existing stations. However, if additional stations are ever installed in the NETN, the primary goals should be: (a) to add redundancy as backup for loss of data from current stations (or loss of the physical stations) and (b) to provide added information on spatial heterogeneity in climate arising from local-scale climate variations arising from heterogeneous land cover and/or topographic diversity.

5.3. Climate Change Detection

The eastern U.S. has the greatest number of long-term climate stations in the nation, stations that are valuable in monitoring climate changes. The desire for credible, accurate, complete, and long-term climate records—from any location—cannot be overemphasized. Thus, this consideration always should have a high priority. However, because of spatial diversity in climate, monitoring that fills knowledge gaps and provides information on long-term temporal variability in short-distance relationships also will be valuable.

5.4. Aesthetics

This issue arises frequently enough to deserve comment. Standards for quality climate measurements require open exposures away from heat sources, buildings, pavement, close vegetation and tall trees, and human intrusion (thus away from property lines). By their nature, sites that meet these standards are usually quite visible. In many settings (such as heavily forested areas) these sites also are quite rare, making them precisely the same places that managers wish to protect from aesthetic intrusion. The most suitable and scientifically defensible sites frequently are rejected as candidate locations for weather/climate stations. Most weather/climate stations, therefore, tend to be "hidden" but many of these hidden locations have inferior exposures. Some measure of compromise is nearly always called for when siting weather and climate stations.

The public has vast interest and curiosity in weather and climate, and within the NPS I&M networks, such measurements consistently rate near or at the top of desired public information. There seem to be many possible opportunities for exploiting and embracing this widespread interest within the interpretive mission of the NPS. One way to do this would be to highlight rather than hide these stations and educate the public about the need for adequate siting. A number of weather displays we have encountered during visits have proven inadvertently to serve as counterexamples for how measurements should not be made.

5.5. Information Access

Access to information promotes its use, which in turn promotes attention to station care and maintenance, better data, and more use. An end-to-end view that extends from sensing to decision support is far preferable to isolated and disconnected activities and aids the support infrastructure that is ultimately so necessary for successful, long-term climate monitoring.

Decisions about improvements in monitoring capacity are facilitated greatly by the ability to examine available climate information. Various methods are being created at WRCC to improve access to that information. Web pages providing historic and ongoing climate data, and information from NETN park units can be accessed at http://www.wrcc.dri.edu/nps. In the event that this URL changes, there still will be links from the main WRCC Web page entitled "Projects" under NPS.

The WRCC has been steadily developing software to summarize data from hourly sites. This has been occurring under the aegis of the RAWS program and a growing array of product generators ranging from daily and monthly data lists to wind roses and hourly frequency distributions. All park data are available to park personnel via an access code (needed only for data listings) that can be acquired by request. The WRCC RAWS Web page is located at http://www.wrcc.dri.edu/wraws or http://www.raws.dri.edu.

Web pages have been developed to provide access not only to historic and ongoing climate data and information from NETN park units but also to climate-monitoring efforts for NETN. These pages can be found through http://www.wrcc.dri.edu/nps.

Additional access to more standard climate information is accessible though the previously mentioned Web pages, as well as through http://www.wrcc.dri.edu/summary. These summaries are generally for COOP stations.

5.6. Summarized Conclusions and Recommendations

- NETN climate is influenced by its proximity to the Atlantic Ocean, which helps to explain significant coast-interior gradients in temperature and precipitation.
- Extreme events such as ice storms and tropical systems are a primary means of introducing disturbances into the temperate hardwood forest ecosystems of the NETN.
- Spatial patterns in land use strongly influence local climate characteristics in the NETN.
- NETN park units generally must rely on sources of weather/climate data that are outside of the park units. Reliable long-term COOP stations and SAO stations at major airports are generally available.
- Despite its location in the western suburbs of New York City, MORR has only one active site within 10 km of the park unit. Otherwise, the closest reliable near-real-time data comes from SAO sites at least 30 km to the east of MORR, at the international airports in and around New York City.
- The COOP station that is currently active in Acadia National Park should continue operation. Partnerships between NPS and local NWS offices can be valuable towards this objective.

6.0 Literature Cited

American Association of State Climatologists. 1985. Heights and exposure standards for sensors on automated weather stations. The State Climatologist **9**.

Bevis, M., S. Businger, T. A. Herring, C. Rocken, R. A. Anthes, and R. H. Ware. 1992. GPS meteorology: remote sensing of the atmospheric water vapor using the global positioning system. Journal of Geophysical Research **97**:75–94.

Bonan, G. B. 2002. Ecological Climatology: Concepts and Applications. Cambridge University Press.

Boose E. R., K. E. Chamberlin, and D. R. Foster. 2001. Landscape and regional impacts of hurricanes in New England. Ecological Monographs **71**:27–48.

Brooks, R. T. 2004. Weather-related effects on woodland vernal pool hydrology and hydroperiod. Wetlands **24**:104-114.

Bureau of Land Management. 1997. Remote Automatic Weather Station (RAWS) and Remote Environmental Monitoring Systems (REMS) standards. RAWS/REMS Support Facility, Boise, Idaho.

Changnon, S. A. 2003. Characteristics of ice storms in the United States. Journal of Applied Meteorology **42**:630–639.

Changnon, S. A., and T. R. Karl. 2003. Temporal and spatial variations of freezing rain in the contiguous United States: 1948–2000. Journal of Applied Meteorology **42**:1302–1315.

Chapin III, F. S., M. S. Torn, and M. Tateno. 1996. Principles of ecosystem sustainability. The American Naturalist **148**:1016-1037.

Cooter, E. J., and S. K. Leduc. 1995. Recent frost date trends in the northeastern USA. International Journal of Climatology **15**:65-75.

Curtis, P. S., and X. Z. Wang. 1998. A meta-analysis of elevated CO_2 effects on woody plant mass, form, and physiology. Oecologia **113**:299-313.

Daly, C., R. P. Neilson, and D. L. Phillips. 1994. A statistical-topographic model for mapping climatological precipitation over mountainous terrain. Journal of Applied Meteorology **33**:140-158.

Daly, C., W. P. Gibson, G. H. Taylor, G. L. Johnson, and P. Pasteris. 2002. A knowledge-based approach to the statistical mapping of climate. Climate Research **22**:99-113.

Darwin, A. T., D. Ladd, R. Galdins, T. A. Contreras, and L. Fahrig. 2004. Response of forest understory vegetation to a major ice storm. Journal of the Torrey Botanical Society **131**:45-52.

DeGaetano, A. T. 2000. Climatic perspective and impacts of the 1998 northern New York and New England ice storm. Bulletin of the American Meteorological Society **81**:237-254.

Doggett, M., C. Daly, J. Smith, W. Gibson, G. Taylor, G. Johnson, and P. Pasteris. 2004. High-resolution 1971-2000 mean monthly temperature maps for the western United States. Fourteenth AMS Conf. on Applied Climatology, 84th AMS Annual Meeting. Seattle, Washington, American Meteorological Society, Boston, Massachusetts, January 2004, Paper 4.3, CD-ROM.

Duan, J., M. Bevis, P. Fang, Y. Bock, S. Chiswell, S. Businger, C. Rocken, F. Solheim, T. van Hove, R. Ware, and others. 1996. GPS meteorology: direct estimation of the absolute value of precipitable water. Journal of Applied Meteorology 35:830-838.

Dudley R. W., and G. A. Hodgkins. 2002. Trends in streamflow, river ice, and snowpack for coastal river basins in Maine during the 20th Century. Maine USGS report WRIR02-4245, 26 p.

Environmental Protection Agency. 1987. On-site meteorological program guidance for regulatory modeling applications. EPA-450/4-87-013. Environmental Protection Agency, Office of Air Quality Planning and Standards, Research Triangle Park, North Carolina.

Finklin, A. I., and W. C. Fischer. 1990. Weather station handbook –an interagency guide for wildland managers. NFES No. 2140. National Wildfire Coordinating Group, Boise, Idaho.

Gibbs, J. P., and W. G. Shriver. 2002. Estimating the effects of road mortality on turtle populations. Conservation Biology **16**:1647-1652.

Gibson, W. P., C. Daly, T. Kittel, D. Nychka, C. Johns, N. Rosenbloom, A. McNab, and G. Taylor. 2002. Development of a 103-year high-resolution climate data set for the conterminous United States. Thirteenth AMS Conf. on Applied Climatology. Portland, Oregon, American Meteorological Society, Boston, MA, May 2002:181-183.

Groisman P. Ya., R. W. Knight, and T. R. Karl. 2000. Heavy precipitation and high streamflow in the contiguous United States: trends in the 20th Century. Bulletin of the American Meteorological Society **82**:219-246.

Hannah, L., J. L. Carr, and A. Lankeerani. 1995. Human disturbance and natural habitat: a biome level analysis of a global data set. Biodiversity and Conservation **4**:128-155.

Hodgkins, G. A., R. W. Dudley, and T. G. Huntington. 2003. Changes in the timing of high river flow in New England over the 20th Century. Journal of Hydrology **278**:244-252.

Hurrell, J. W. 1995. Decadal trends in the North Atlantic Oscillation: regional temperatures and precipitation. Science **269**:676–679.

Hurrell, J. W., and H. van Loon. 1997. Decadal variations in climate associated with the North Atlantic Oscillation. Climatic Change **36**:301–326.

Hynes, H. B. N. 1975. The ecology of running water: Toronto, University of Toronto Press.

I&M. 2006. I&M Inventories home page. http://science.nature.nps.gov/im/inventory/index.cfm.

IPCC. 2002. Intergovernmental Panel on Climate Change: Climate Change and Biodiversity. V.

Irland, L. C. 1998. Ice storm 1998 and the forests of the Northeast: a preliminary assessment. Journal of Forestry **96**:32-40

Jacobson, M. C., R. J. Charlson, H. Rodhe, and G. H. Orians. 2000. Earth System Science: From Biogeochemical Cycles to Global Change. Academic Press, San Diego.

Johnson, D. W., R. B. Thomas, K. L. Griffin, D. T. Tissue, J. T. Ball, B. R. Strain, and R. F. Walker. 1998. Effects of carbon dioxide and nitrogen on growth and nitrogen uptake in ponderosa and loblolly pine. Journal of Environmental Quality **27**:414-425.

Karl, T. R., V. E. Derr, D. R. Easterling, C. K. Folland, D. J. Hoffman, S. Levitus, N. Nicholls, D. E. Parker, and G. W. Withee. 1996a. Critical issues for long-term climate monitoring. Pages 55-92 *in* T. R. Karl, editor. Long Term Climate Monitoring by the Global Climate Observing System, Kluwer Publishing.

Karl, T. R., R. W. Knight, D. R. Easterling, and R. G. Quayle, 1996b. Trends in U.S. climate during the twentieth century. Consequences **1**:2-12.

Karl, T. R., and R. W. Knight. 1998. Secular trends in precipitation amount, frequency, and intensity in the United States. Bull. Amer. Meteor. Soc. **79**:231-241.

Kidder, S. Q., and T. H. Vonder Haar. 1995. Satellite Meteorology: An Introduction. Academic Press, San Diego.

Kraft C. E., R. L. Schneider, and D. R. Warren. 2002. Ice storm impacts on woody debris and debris dam formation in northeastern U.S. streams. Canadian Journal of Fisheries and Aquatic Sciences **59**:1677–1684.

Long, S. P., C. P. Osborne, and S. W. Humphries. 1996. Photosynthesis, rising atmospheric carbon dioxide concentration and climate change. *in* A. I. Breymeyer, D. O. Hall, J. M. Melillo, and G. I. Ågren, editors. Global Change: Effects on Coniferous Forests and Grasslands. John Wiley and Sons, New York.

Millward, A. A., and C. E. Kraft. 2004. Physical influences of landscape on a large-extent ecological disturbance: the northeastern North American ice storm of 1998. Landscape Ecology **19**: 99–111.

National Assessment Synthesis Team. 2001. Climate Change Impacts on the United States: The Potential Consequences of Climate Variability and Change, Report for the U.S. Global Change Research Program. Cambridge University Press, Cambridge, UK.

National Research Council. 2001. A Climate Services Vision: First Steps Toward the Future. National Academies Press, Washington, D.C.

National Wildfire Coordinating Group. 2004. National fire danger rating system weather station standards. Report PMS 426.3. National Wildfire Coordinating Group, Boise, Idaho.

Neilson, R. P. 1987. Biotic regionalization and climatic controls in western North America. Vegetatio **70**:135-147.

New England Regional Assessment Group. 2001. Preparing for a Changing climate: the potential consequences of climate variability and change: New England Regional Overview. University of New Hampshire.

Oakley, K. L., L. P. Thomas, and S. G. Fancy. 2003. Guidelines for long-term monitoring protocols. Wildlife Society Bulletin **31**:1000-1003.

Pasher, J., and D. J. King. 2006. Landscape fragmentation and ice storm damage in eastern Ontario forests. Landscape Ecology **31**:477-483.

Poff, N. L. 1997. Landscape filters and species traits; towards a mechanistic understanding and prediction in stream ecology: Journal of the North American Benthological Society **16**:391-409.

Rey, A., and P. G. Jarvis. 1998. Long-term photosynthetic acclimation to increased atmospheric CO_2 concentration in young birch (Betula pendula) trees. Tree Physiology **18**:441-450.

Root, T. L., and S. H. Schneider. 2002. Climate change: overview and implications for wildlife. Pages 437 *in* S. H. Schneider and T. L. Root, editors. Wildlife Responses to Climate Change: North American Case Studies. Island Press, Washington, DC.

Schlesinger, W. H. 1997. Biogeochemistry: An Analysis of Global Change. Academic Press, San Diego.

Schwartz, M. D., and B. E. Reiter. 2000. Changes in North American spring. International Journal of Climatology **20**:929-932.

Shriver, W. G., B. R. Mitchell, F. Dieffenbach, D. Faber-Langendoen, G. Tierney, P. Lombard, T. Moore, and J. Gibbs. 2005. Northeast Temperate Network Vital Signs Monitoring Plan. National Park Service, Northeast Temperate Network, Woodstock, Vermont.

Smith, E. 1999. Atlantic and East Coast hurricanes 1900-98: a frequency and intensity study for the twenty-first century. Bulletin of the American Meteorological Society **80**:2717-2720.

Steen, D. A., and J. P. Gibbs. 2004. Effects of roads on the structure of freshwater turtle populations. Conservation Biology **18**:1149-1153.

Tanner, B. D. 1990. Automated weather stations. Remote Sensing Reviews **5**:73-98.

Thompson, D. W. J., and J. M. Wallace. 1998. The Arctic Oscillation signature in the wintertime geopotential height and temperature fields. Geophysical Research Letters **25**:1297–1300.

Trombulak, S. C., and C. A. Frissell. 2000. Review of ecological effects of roads on terrestrial and aquatic communities. Conservation Biology **14**:18-30.

Wettstein, J. J., and L. O. Mearns. 2002. The influence of the North Atlantic–Arctic Oscillation on mean, variance, and extremes of temperature in the northeastern United States and Canada. Journal of Climate **15**:3586-3600.

World Meteorological Organization. 1983. Guide to meteorological instruments and methods of observation, No. 8, 5th edition, World Meteorological Organization, Geneva Switzerland.

World Meteorological Organization. 2005. Organization and planning of intercomparisons of rainfall intensity gauges. World Meteorological Organization, Geneva Switzerland.

Yuan, L. L., R. A. Anthes, R. H. Ware, C. Rocken, W. D. Bonner, M. G. Bevis, and S. Businger. 1993. Sensing climate change using the global positioning system. Journal of Geophysical Research **98**:14,925-14,937.

Appendix A. Appalachian National Scenic Trail

A.1. Background

The Appalachian National Scenic Trail (APPA) was established by Congress in 1968 as one of the first National Scenic Trails. This continuously-marked footpath extends approximately 2,175 miles across the Appalachian Mountains from Georgia to Maine. The entire APPA is a unit of NPS, administered broadly by NPS and managed cooperatively by over 105 agencies and organizations.

A.2. Station Locations

We have conducted an inventory of weather/climate stations for the APPA. Stations from seven weather/climate networks have been included in this inventory (Table A.1). Stations within 20 km of the administrative boundaries of APPA were considered. This report only includes those COOP stations having at least 50 years of data, in an attempt to emphasize COOP stations having long-term climate records. In some circumstances, stations that are greater than 20 km away from the boundaries of APPA are included from the Soil Climate Analysis Network (SCAN) and NPS air quality monitoring programs such as CASTNet, GPMP, and the Portable Ozone Monitoring System (POMS). This is true in particular for sites that are west of APPA, as these sites are generally upwind of APPA and play an important role in monitoring fluxes of air pollutants into APPA. Some historical stations from the main air quality monitoring programs are also included.

Table A.1. Weather/climate networks for APPA.

Acronym	Name
CASTNet	Clean Air Status and Trends Network
COOP	NWS Cooperative Observer Program
GPMP	Gaseous Pollutant Monitoring Program
POMS	Portable Ozone Monitoring System
RAWS	Remote Automated Weather Station network
SAO	NWS/FAA Surface Airways Observation Network
SCAN	Soil Climate Analysis Network

A.2.1. Southern APPA

We have identified five CASTNet stations for the southern segment of APPA (Table A.2). These stations are either at or west of the APPA (Figure A.1). The two CASTNet stations located closest to the APPA are "Cowetta" and "Cranberry." "Coweeta" is located a couple of kilometers east of APPA and just north of the Georgia/North Carolina border. "Cranberry" is located just about 2 km southeast of APPA, about 10 km west of Banner Elk, North Carolina.

The GPMP sites we identified for this segment of APPA (Table A.2) are all located in Great Smoky Mountains National Park (GRSM). The most relevant GPMP station for APPA is the station "Clingman's Dome," located right on the trail (Figure A.1) and just north of the Georgia/North Carolina border. The GPMP sites at Purchase Knob (eastern GRSM) and Cove

Mountain (just north of Elkmont in northern GRSM) also provide higher-elevation weather data that is representative of the areas through which APPA passes.

Several RAWS stations provide near-real-time weather data within 20 km of APPA. Although RAWS stations are located near the entire southern segment of APPA, most of the RAWS stations in this segment are concentrated in southwestern North Carolina and northern Georgia (Figure A.1). We identified eight SAO stations within 20 km of the southern segment of APPA (Table A.2). Most of these are located at lower-elevation airports.

Table A.2. Weather/climate stations for the southern segment of APPA, from Georgia to the North Carolina/Virginia border. Missing entries are indicated by "M".

Name	Lat.	Lon.	Elev. (m)	Network	Start	End
Coweeta	35.061	-83.431	686	CASTNet	11/1/1987	Present
Cranberry	36.106	-82.045	1219	CASTNet	12/1/1988	Present
Look Rock	35.633	-83.942	793	CASTNet	7/1/1988	Present
Oak Ridge	35.960	-84.290	341	CASTNet	1/1/1987	12/1/1988
Speedwell	36.470	-83.827	361	CASTNet	6/1/1989	Present
Ashford	35.892	-81.935	546	COOP	5/27/1942	Present
Banner Elk	36.153	-81.863	1142	COOP	9/1/1907	Present
Barnardsville 2 SE	35.760	-82.433	707	COOP	1/1/1949	Present
Blowing Rock 1 NW	36.147	-81.703	1173	COOP	1/1/1893	Present
Bristol Tri City Airport	36.473	-82.404	457	COOP	7/1/1934	Present
Cataloochee	35.638	-83.096	808	COOP	1/1/1949	Present
Celo 2 S	35.830	-82.177	817	COOP	8/1/1948	Present
Cleveland	34.588	-83.768	478	COOP	4/1/1943	Present
Coweeta Exp. Stn.	35.059	-83.431	685	COOP	12/1/1942	Present
Elizabethton	36.364	-82.233	535	COOP	4/1/1895	Present
Gatlinburg 2 SW	35.688	-83.537	443	COOP	12/1/1921	Present
Grandfather Mountain	36.109	-81.833	1615	COOP	8/1/1955	Present
Greeneville Exp. Stn.	36.106	-82.844	402	COOP	5/1/1890	Present
Haw Knob	35.350	-84.033	1415	COOP	9/1/1948	Present
Helen	34.700	-83.726	455	COOP	4/1/1956	Present
Helton	36.563	-81.504	866	COOP	3/1/1940	Present
Hot Springs	35.895	-82.831	426	COOP	1/1/1927	Present
Jasper 1 NNW	34.496	-84.459	447	COOP	6/1/1937	Present
Jefferson 2 E	36.416	-81.429	844	COOP	2/1/1896	Present
Marshall	35.804	-82.666	610	COOP	11/1/1898	Present
Mountain City 2	36.476	-81.792	765	COOP	1/1/1956	Present
Newport 1 NW	35.983	-83.201	316	COOP	8/1/1891	Present
Spruce Pine	35.900	-82.067	796	COOP	1/1/1949	Present
Tapoco	35.456	-83.940	338	COOP	9/1/1929	Present
Transou	36.392	-81.304	876	COOP	4/1/1946	Present
Trout Dale 3 SSW	36.660	-81.405	860	COOP	8/1/1948	Present
Waterville 2	35.774	-83.098	439	COOP	8/1/1948	Present
Cades Cove	35.604	-83.783	564	GPMP	7/1/1993	Present

Name	Lat.	Lon.	Elev. (m)	Network	Start	End
Clingmans Dome	35.562	-83.498	2021	GPMP	10/2/1992	Present
Cove Mountain	35.697	-83.609	1243	GPMP	7/1/1988	Present
Elkmont	35.664	-83.590	640	GPMP	7/1/1980	9/30/1983
Look Rock	35.633	-83.942	793	GPMP	7/1/1988	4/27/1996
Purchase Knob	35.590	-83.078	1500	GPMP	6/1/1995	Present
Twin Creeks	35.686	-83.501	610	GPMP	6/1/1993	8/31/1993
Carl Sandburg	35.265	-82.451	M	POMS	7/14/2005	Present
Cumberland Gap Pinnacles	36.606	-83.665	749	POMS	6/1/2005	6/22/2005
7 Mile Ridge	35.803	-82.650	662	RAWS	1/1/2004	Present
Brasstown #1	34.803	-83.710	1000	RAWS	8/1/2001	Present
Camp Merrill	34.630	-84.098	531	RAWS	11/1/2001	Present
Chattooga #1	34.640	-83.522	457	RAWS	8/1/2001	Present
Cheoah	35.333	-83.817	640	RAWS	2/1/2003	Present
Cherokee	35.620	-83.207	1036	RAWS	2/1/2002	Present
Highlands	35.084	-83.218	1158	RAWS	2/1/2003	Present
Indian Grave	35.624	-83.808	823	RAWS	2/1/1997	Present
Laurel Springs	36.400	-81.283	914	RAWS	10/1/2002	Present
Stackrock Creek (FR2) North	36.070	-81.799	884	RAWS	12/1/2004	Present
Tallulah #1	34.906	-83.334	831	RAWS	8/1/2001	Present
Tusquitee	35.040	-84.060	699	RAWS	2/1/2003	Present
Unicoi	36.133	-82.450	732	RAWS	10/1/2001	Present
Wayah	35.167	-83.403	658	RAWS	2/1/2003	Present
Abingdon Virginia Highlands Arpt.	36.683	-82.033	631	SAO	6/1/1991	Present
Andrews Murphy Arpt.	35.195	-83.865	517	SAO	M	Present
Boone Watauga Co. Hosp.	36.200	-81.650	M	SAO	M	Present
Bristol Tri City Arpt.	36.473	-82.404	457	SAO	7/1/1934	Present
Canton Cherokee Co. Arpt.	34.311	-84.424	372	SAO	3/15/2004	Present
Gainesville Lee Gilmer Mem. Arpt.	34.272	-83.830	389	SAO	10/17/1995	Present
Jefferson Ashe Co. Arpt.	36.432	-81.419	969	SAO	M	Present
Macon Co. Arpt.	35.223	-83.419	616	SAO	1/1/2004	Present
Reynolds Homestead	36.630	-80.130	344	SCAN	M	Present
Watkinsville #1	33.880	-83.430	235	SCAN	M	Present

Of the COOP stations that we identified within 20 km of APPA, six have data records reaching back into the 1890s (Table A.2). Of these stations, the most reliable data records come from "Greeneville Exp. Stn.," "Marshall," and "Newport 1 NW." The COOP stations "Greeneville Exp. Stn." and "Newport 1 NW" are both located 20 km northwest of APPA, in the foothills of eastern Tennessee. "Marshall," on the other hand, is located 15 km southeast of APPA, about 40 km east of GRSM and 30 km north of Asheville. West of Marshall, the COOP station "Waterville 2" is located within a kilometer of the APPA at the eastern boundary of GRSM, along the North Carolina/Tennessee border (Figure A.1).

Figure A.1. Station locations for the southern segment of APPA.

55

The data record from this station is very complete. Other higher-elevation COOP stations within 20 km of the southern segment of APPA include "Banner Elk" and "Grandfather Mountain," in northwestern North Carolina. "Banner Elk" is less than 10 km east of APPA, while "Grandfather Mountain" is almost 20 km east of APPA, along the Blue Ridge Parkway. Both of these stations have reliable data records, although "Banner Elk" has been less reliable since the mid-1990s.

A.2.2. Mid-Atlantic APPA

Eight CASTNet stations, seven of which are still active, have been identified for the mid-Atlantic segment of APPA (Table A.3). Three of these stations are located within five kilometers of APPA. "Horton Stn.," near Blacksburg, Virginia is less than five kilometers southeast of APPA. "Arendtsville" is less than five kilometers southeast of APPA in southern Pennsylvania. "Big Meadows" in Shenandoah National Park (SHEN) is within a kilometer of the trail, near the Big Meadows visitor center. A COOP station operated nearby until 2003.

We identified three RAWS stations along the mid-Atlantic segment of APPA (Table A.3). These are all located in either southwestern Virginia or southern West Virginia (Figure A.2). The closest RAWS station, "Craig Valley," is only about five kilometers north of APPA.

In addition to these RAWS stations, there are numerous SAO stations providing near-real-time weather data along the mid-Atlantic segment of APPA. Most of these stations are located at local and regional airports. The SAO stations with the longest data records are "Harrisburg Capital City Arpt." (1926-present) and "Martinsburg E WV Reg." (1926-present). Three SAO stations are particularly close to APPA. "Roanoke Reg. Arpt." is about 10 km south of APPA and has been operating since 1934. "Muir AAF" is only about five kilometers south of APPA and has been operating since 1978. However, the closest SAO station to APPA is "Camp David Thurmont" in northern Maryland, less than five kilometers east of APPA.

There are numerous long-term COOP stations located within 20 km of APPA in the mid-Atlantic region. In fact, many of the data records go back to the 1800s and early 1900s. Three of these stations are located very close to APPA. The COOP station "Burkes Garden," located three kilometers north of APPA in southwestern Virginia, has a data record that starts in 1896 and is very complete. "Buchanan" is a COOP station located about 10 km northwest of APPA, 30 km northeast of Roanoke. This station started in 1892 and has a fairly complete record with the exception of a significant data gap from April, 1985 to May, 1989. The COOP station "Harpers Ferry River" is within two kilometers of APPA. This station's data record begins in 1889 but is of questionable quality. Additional reliable COOP stations are located very close to APPA in northern Virginia and Pennsylvania. "Mount Weather," about 20 km northeast of SHEN, is located just five kilometers east of APPA and has a reliable data record that goes back to 1915. The COOP station "South Mountain" is located in southern Pennsylvania and is only one kilometer east of APPA. This station's data record is quite reliable and starts in 1940.

Table A.3. Weather/climate stations for the mid-Atlantic segment of APPA, from the North Carolina/Virginia border to Pennsylvania. Missing entries are indicated by "M".

Name	Lat.	Lon.	Elev. (m)	Network	Start	End
Arendtsville	39.923	-77.308	269	CASTNet	6/1/1988	Present
Beltsville	39.028	-76.817	46	CASTNet	11/1/1988	Present

Name	Lat.	Lon.	Elev. (m)	Network	Start	End
Big Meadows	38.523	-78.435	1073	CASTNet	5/1/1983	Present
Horton Station	37.330	-80.558	920	CASTNet	6/1/1987	Present
Penn State University	40.721	-77.932	378	CASTNet	1/1/1987	Present
Prince Edward	37.166	-78.307	150	CASTNet	11/1/1987	Present
Scotia Range	40.788	-77.946	376	CASTNet	2/1/1993	2/1/1999
Washington's Crossing	40.313	-74.873	61	CASTNet	12/1/1988	Present
Alderson	37.727	-80.659	469	COOP	3/1/1944	Present
Allentown Lehigh Valley Intl Arpt.	40.651	-75.449	119	COOP	1/1/1930	Present
Berne River Gage	40.523	-75.999	94	COOP	10/1/1956	Present
Blacksburg NWSO	37.202	-80.413	640	COOP	1/1/1952	Present
Bland	37.100	-81.116	610	COOP	2/1/1944	Present
Bloserville 1 N	40.264	-77.364	213	COOP	11/1/1912	Present
Bluefield Mercer Co. Arpt.	37.296	-81.208	875	COOP	5/1/1954	Present
Bluestone Lake	37.641	-80.883	424	COOP	3/1/1943	Present
Buchanan	37.527	-79.678	264	COOP	11/26/1892	Present
Buena Vista	37.727	-79.363	253	COOP	6/15/1937	Present
Burkes Garden	37.093	-81.336	1006	COOP	3/11/1896	Present
Chambersburg 1 ESE	39.935	-77.639	195	COOP	1/1/1894	Present
Charlottesville 2 W	38.033	-78.523	265	COOP	1/1/1893	Present
Charlottesville Albemarle Arpt.	38.139	-78.453	195	COOP	8/1/1955	Present
Claussville	40.617	-75.650	204	COOP	8/1/1945	Present
Copper Hill	37.086	-80.142	820	COOP	4/1/1940	Present
Dale Enterprise	38.455	-78.935	427	COOP	1/1/1893	Present
Easton 2	40.683	-75.233	52	COOP	11/9/1956	Present
Elizabethville 1 N	40.567	-76.817	158	COOP	12/1/1893	Present
Frederick Mun. Arpt.	39.417	-77.383	94	COOP	10/1/1933	Present
Glen Lyn	37.373	-80.860	463	COOP	3/1/1914	Present
Greenwood Res.	40.833	-75.933	314	COOP	1/8/1942	Present
Hamburg	40.552	-75.995	107	COOP	1/1/1894	Present
Harpers Ferry River	39.323	-77.729	75	COOP	7/1/1889	Present
Harrisburg Capital City Arpt.	40.217	-76.851	104	COOP	1/1/1926	Present
Harrisburg River Gage	40.250	-76.883	88	COOP	11/1/1890	Present
Kerrs Creek 6 WNW	37.871	-79.569	457	COOP	8/1/1948	Present
Lafayette 1 NE	37.239	-80.199	402	COOP	6/1/1951	Present
Lebanon 2 W	40.333	-76.467	137	COOP	5/1/1948	Present
Lehighton 1 SSW	40.822	-75.696	177	COOP	12/20/1934	Present
Lexington	37.795	-79.414	343	COOP	6/1/1889	Present
Lick Run	37.774	-79.785	299	COOP	12/15/1943	Present
Lincoln	39.088	-77.693	152	COOP	9/26/1900	Present
Lindside	37.480	-80.656	605	COOP	4/5/1940	Present
Luray 5 E	38.666	-78.373	427	COOP	3/1/1941	Present

Name	Lat.	Lon.	Elev. (m)	Network	Start	End
Lynchburg 7 St. Br.	37.424	-79.159	171	COOP	1/1/1910	Present
Lynchburg Reg. Arpt.	37.321	-79.207	287	COOP	1/1/1930	Present
Martinsburg E WV Rgnl.	39.402	-77.984	163	COOP	1/1/1926	Present
Middletown Harrisburg Intl. Arpt.	40.194	-76.763	95	COOP	4/1/1928	Present
Midland Park	40.994	-74.145	64	COOP	8/1/1945	Present
Montebello Fish Hatchery	37.849	-79.131	807	COOP	9/1/1948	Present
Mount Weather	39.063	-77.889	524	COOP	1/1/1915	Present
Myerstown	40.368	-76.306	146	COOP	8/18/1938	Present
Newport River	40.478	-77.129	116	COOP	9/1/1924	Present
Pedlar Dam	37.671	-79.279	308	COOP	11/1/1926	Present
Phillipsburg Easton	40.700	-75.200	61	COOP	1/1/1940	Present
Pilot 1 ENE	37.067	-80.350	664	COOP	4/3/1940	Present
Pompton Lakes	40.983	-74.283	62	COOP	10/30/1956	Present
Princeton	37.384	-81.082	722	COOP	6/1/1900	Present
Pulaski	37.056	-80.784	564	COOP	5/1/1920	Present
Pulaski	37.133	-80.683	642	COOP	10/1/1937	Present
Reading Spaatz Field	40.367	-75.967	104	COOP	8/1/1941	Present
Roanoke Reg. Arpt.	37.317	-79.974	358	COOP	7/1/1934	Present
Roanoke River Gage	37.258	-79.939	276	COOP	8/1/1948	Present
Saltville 1 N	36.889	-81.771	528	COOP	12/1/1894	Present
Shermansdale	40.323	-77.169	129	COOP	1/30/1930	Present
Shippensburg	40.050	-77.517	207	COOP	9/1/1910	Present
Somerset	38.246	-78.270	155	COOP	1/1/1945	Present
South Mountain	39.858	-77.477	463	COOP	5/23/1940	Present
Spring Grove	39.867	-76.867	137	COOP	1/1/1932	Present
Staffordsville 3 ENE	37.271	-80.713	594	COOP	9/1/1951	Present
Staunton Sewage Plant	38.181	-79.090	500	COOP	1/1/1893	Present
Strausstown	40.483	-76.183	183	COOP	8/1/1945	Present
Stuarts Draft	38.010	-79.049	442	COOP	11/1/1945	Present
Tamaqua	40.795	-75.975	282	COOP	12/1/1940	Present
The Plains 2 NNE	38.896	-77.755	162	COOP	4/1/1954	Present
Tye River 1 SE	37.638	-78.934	219	COOP	10/13/1937	Present
Union 3 SSE	37.544	-80.534	643	COOP	2/1/1894	Present
Williamsport	39.604	-77.836	110	COOP	11/1/1938	Present
Winchester 7 SE	39.183	-78.117	207	COOP	4/1/1912	Present
Woodstock 2 NE	38.902	-78.475	207	COOP	9/6/1889	Present
Wytheville 1 S	36.932	-81.094	747	COOP	1/1/1893	Present
Big Meadows	38.523	-78.435	1073	GPMP	1/1/1988	7/31/1995
Dickey Ridge	38.857	-78.201	610	GPMP	5/1/1983	10/31/1994
Sawmill Run	38.106	-78.831	445	GPMP	5/1/1983	10/31/1994
Berwind	37.259	-81.698	504	RAWS	12/1/2004	Present
Craig Valley	37.522	-80.080	386	RAWS	5/1/1998	Present

Name	Lat.	Lon.	Elev. (m)	Network	Start	End
Pipestem	37.526	-80.999	831	RAWS	12/1/2004	Present
Allentown Lehigh Valley Intl. Arpt.	40.651	-75.449	119	SAO	1/1/1930	Present
Belvidere River	40.833	-75.083	70	SAO	9/1/1976	Present
Blacksburg NWSO	37.202	-80.413	640	SAO	1/1/1952	Present
Blacksburg Virginia Tech Arpt.	37.208	-80.408	650	SAO	M	Present
Bluefield Mercer Co. Arpt.	37.296	-81.208	875	SAO	5/1/1954	Present
Camp David Thurmont	39.650	-77.467	569	SAO	M	Present
Charlottesville Albemarle Arpt.	38.139	-78.453	195	SAO	8/1/1955	Present
Frederick Municipal Arpt.	39.417	-77.383	94	SAO	10/1/1933	Present
Hagerstown Washington Co. Reg.	39.708	-77.730	213	SAO	1/1/1931	Present
Harrisburg	40.167	-77.333	0	SAO	M	Present
Harrisburg Capital City Arpt.	40.217	-76.851	104	SAO	1/1/1926	Present
Kutztown Airport	40.500	-75.783	156	SAO	4/1/1994	Present
Leesburg Exec. Arpt.	39.078	-77.558	119	SAO	M	Present
Lynchburg Regional Arpt.	37.321	-79.207	287	SAO	1/1/1930	Present
Martinsburg E WV Reg.	39.402	-77.984	163	SAO	1/1/1926	Present
Middletown Harrisburg Intl. Arpt.	40.194	-76.763	95	SAO	4/1/1928	Present
Mountain Empire Arpt.	36.895	-81.350	780	SAO	3/1/1992	Present
Muir AAF	40.433	-76.567	149	SAO	8/1/1978	Present
Pulaski	37.133	-80.683	642	SAO	10/1/1937	Present
Reading Spaatz Field	40.367	-75.967	104	SAO	8/1/1941	Present
Richlands Tazewell Arpt.	37.064	-81.798	808	SAO	8/29/2002	Present
Roanoke Reg. Arpt.	37.317	-79.974	358	SAO	7/1/1934	Present
Staunton	38.264	-78.896	362	SAO	2/1/1960	Present
Winchester Reg. Arpt.	39.143	-78.144	222	SAO	11/1/1991	Present
York Airport	39.918	-76.874	148	SAO	4/1/1975	Present
Mahantango Ck.	40.670	-76.670	223	SCAN	M	Present
N Piedmont AREC	38.230	-78.120	158	SCAN	M	Present
Powder Mill	39.020	-76.850	32	SCAN	M	Present
Rock Springs PA	40.720	-77.930	372	SCAN	M	Present
Shenandoah	37.920	-79.200	537	SCAN	M	Present

Figure A.2. Station locations for the mid-Atlantic segment of APPA.

A.2.3. Northern APPA

Eight CASTNet stations, five of which are still active, have been identified for the northern segment of APPA (Table A.4). One of these stations, "Lye Brook," is located within a kilometer of APPA in southern Vermont. There is also a SCAN station at this location (also called "Lye Brook"). Other SCAN sites within 5-10 km of APPA include "Hubbard Brook," in north-central New Hampshire, and "Mascoma River," in west-central New Hampshire (Figure A.3).

Table A.4. Weather/climate stations for the northern segment of APPA, from Pennsylvania to Maine. Missing entries are indicated by "M".

Name	Lat.	Lon.	Elev. (m)	Network	Start	End
Ashland	46.604	-68.414	235	CASTNet	12/1/1988	Present
Claryville	41.942	-74.552	765	CASTNet	5/1/1994	Present
Howland	45.216	-68.708	69	CASTNet	11/1/1992	Present
Hubbard Brook Special	43.950	-71.700	250	CASTNet	6/1/1991	10/1/1994
Lye Brook	43.051	-73.061	730	CASTNet	3/1/1994	Present
West Point-A	41.350	-74.050	203	CASTNet	1/1/1987	9/1/1988
West Point-B	41.350	-74.050	203	CASTNet	1/1/1987	9/1/1993
Woodstock	43.945	-71.701	258	CASTNet	12/1/1988	Present
Bakersville	41.842	-73.009	209	COOP	6/1/1948	Present
Barryville 6 NW	41.500	-74.983	183	COOP	11/5/1956	Present
Berlin	44.450	-71.183	283	COOP	6/1/1886	Present
Berlin Mun. Arpt.	44.576	-71.179	353	COOP	6/1/1951	Present
Bulls Bridge Dam	41.650	-73.483	79	COOP	6/1/1948	Present
Canistear Res.	41.109	-74.482	335	COOP	8/1/1948	Present
Cavendish	43.385	-72.599	257	COOP	2/17/1903	Present
Charlotteburg Res.	41.035	-74.423	232	COOP	4/1/1893	Present
Chittenden	43.706	-72.962	323	COOP	1/1/1904	Present
Corinth	44.041	-72.236	337	COOP	6/1/1948	Present
Danbury	41.400	-73.417	123	COOP	10/1/1937	Present
Dover Foxcroft 2	45.183	-69.317	109	COOP	8/1/1902	Present
Eagle Bridge 2 SE	42.933	-73.367	116	COOP	10/19/1951	Present
Errol	44.783	-71.133	390	COOP	1/1/1927	Present
Eustis	45.217	-70.483	384	COOP	11/1/1910	Present
Falls Village	41.950	-73.367	168	COOP	2/1/1916	Present
Gardnerville	41.346	-74.487	140	COOP	10/1/1956	Present
Gilman	44.411	-71.719	256	COOP	5/1/1930	Present
Grafton	42.783	-73.467	475	COOP	8/1/1950	Present
Grafton	43.567	-71.950	253	COOP	12/1/1884	Present
Grafton 1 NW	43.191	-72.625	358	COOP	6/1/1948	Present
Greenville Maine Forestry SVC	45.462	-69.595	313	COOP	10/1/1907	Present
Greenwood Lake	41.139	-74.324	143	COOP	1/1/1941	Present
Hanover	43.700	-72.283	184	COOP	11/1/1884	Present
Lancaster	44.483	-71.583	262	COOP	10/1/1892	Present
Lebanon Mun. Arpt.	43.626	-72.305	181	COOP	7/1/1943	Present

Name	Lat.	Lon.	Elev. (m)	Network	Start	End
Long Falls Dam	45.217	-70.200	354	COOP	7/1/1951	Present
Macopin Lwr. Intk. Dam	41.017	-74.400	177	COOP	1/1/1941	Present
Matamoras	41.367	-74.700	128	COOP	10/1/1904	Present
Middle Dam	44.783	-70.917	445	COOP	4/1/1926	Present
Middletown 2 NW	41.460	-74.449	213	COOP	1/1/1893	Present
Millbrook	41.850	-73.617	250	COOP	11/20/1941	Present
Millinocket	45.650	-68.705	110	COOP	11/1/1902	Present
Millinocket Mun. Arpt.	45.648	-68.686	124	COOP	4/1/1938	Present
Milo	45.256	-69.010	128	COOP	10/1/1921	Present
Moosehead	45.583	-69.717	313	COOP	9/1/1930	Present
Mount Washington	44.267	-71.300	1909	COOP	1/1/1937	Present
Norfolk 2 SW	41.973	-73.221	408	COOP	11/1/1884	Present
N. Adams Harriman-And-West	42.696	-73.171	199	COOP	2/1/1950	Present
North Conway	44.054	-71.127	162	COOP	9/1/1947	Present
Oak Ridge Res.	41.004	-74.499	268	COOP	1/1/1941	Present
Peru	43.267	-72.900	518	COOP	11/1/1940	Present
Pinkham Notch	44.267	-71.250	612	COOP	1/1/1930	Present
Pittsfield Mun. Arpt.	42.427	-73.289	364	COOP	6/1/1925	Present
Plymouth	43.783	-71.650	201	COOP	5/1/1951	Present
Port Jervis	41.380	-74.685	143	COOP	1/1/1893	Present
Poughkeepsie Dutchess Co. Arpt.	41.627	-73.884	51	COOP	12/1/1932	Present
Ringwood	41.092	-74.268	93	COOP	1/1/1902	Present
Rochester	43.863	-72.808	253	COOP	11/1/1928	Present
Rock Hill 3 SW	41.583	-74.617	387	COOP	11/1/1956	Present
Rocky River Dam	41.583	-73.433	67	COOP	6/1/1948	Present
Round Pond	41.301	-73.537	244	COOP	6/1/1948	Present
Rumford 1 SSE	44.533	-70.533	192	COOP	1/16/1943	Present
Rutland	43.617	-72.967	189	COOP	8/18/1916	Present
South Newbury	44.052	-72.081	143	COOP	10/1/1936	Present
Stewart Field	41.500	-74.100	177	COOP	8/1/1942	Present
Stroudsburg	41.013	-75.191	140	COOP	12/1/1910	Present
Sussex 2 NE	41.226	-74.571	137	COOP	1/1/1893	Present
Tannersville 2 E	41.054	-75.290	277	COOP	8/1/1925	Present
Thomaston	41.650	-73.083	116	COOP	1/1/1956	Present
Tobyhanna Pocono Mtn. A	41.139	-75.223	584	COOP	9/12/1901	Present
Union Village Dam	43.797	-72.264	140	COOP	4/1/1950	Present
Upper Dam	44.867	-70.867	451	COOP	6/1/1948	Present
Wanaque Raymond Dam	41.044	-74.293	75	COOP	8/1/1945	Present
Wappingers Falls	41.650	-73.867	35	COOP	3/1/1893	Present
Warren	43.910	-71.888	216	COOP	8/6/1942	Present
Wentworth	43.952	-71.916	189	COOP	9/1/1944	Present
West Hartford 2	43.717	-72.417	114	COOP	4/1/1949	Present

Name	Lat.	Lon.	Elev. (m)	Network	Start	End
West Otis	42.182	-73.224	395	COOP	3/1/1926	Present
West Point	41.391	-73.961	98	COOP	3/1/1890	Present
Woodcliff Lake	41.014	-74.043	31	COOP	7/1/1919	Present
Woodstock	43.622	-72.454	183	COOP	10/1/1892	Present
York Pond	44.500	-71.333	466	COOP	1/11/1931	Present
Steamtown	41.407	-75.668	223	GPMP	4/1/1990	1/31/1992
Hudson Highlands	41.351	-74.048	91	RAWS	8/1/2004	Present
Loch Lomond	41.204	-74.890	274	RAWS	11/1/2004	Present
Marlboro College	42.838	-72.735	514	RAWS	5/1/2003	Present
Ringwood	41.118	-74.240	173	RAWS	10/1/2004	Present
Stonykill	41.500	-73.900	61	RAWS	5/1/2003	Present
Sweezy	43.333	-73.033	204	RAWS	7/1/1999	Present
White Mountain NF	43.981	-71.141	140	RAWS	3/1/2003	Present
Aeroflex-Andover Arpt.	41.009	-74.737	178	SAO	8/17/1998	Present
Bennington Morse State Arpt.	42.891	-73.247	252	SAO	2/1/1968	Present
Berlin Mun. Arpt.	44.576	-71.179	353	SAO	6/1/1951	Present
Danbury Mun. Arpt.	41.371	-73.483	139	SAO	5/1/1973	Present
Greenville Maine Forestry SVC	45.462	-69.595	313	SAO	10/1/1907	Present
Lebanon Mun. Arpt.	43.626	-72.305	181	SAO	7/1/1943	Present
Millinocket Mun. Arpt.	45.648	-68.686	124	SAO	4/1/1938	Present
Montgomery Orange Co. Arpt.	41.509	-74.265	111	SAO	3/1/1972	Present
Mount Pocono Pocono Mtns.	41.139	-75.379	584	SAO	9/29/1999	Present
Mount Washington	44.267	-71.300	1909	SAO	1/1/1937	Present
N. Adams Harriman-And-West	42.696	-73.171	199	SAO	2/1/1950	Present
Pittsfield Mun. Arpt.	42.427	-73.289	364	SAO	6/1/1925	Present
Poughkeepsie Dutchess Co. Arpt.	41.627	-73.884	51	SAO	12/1/1932	Present
Rumford	44.533	-70.533	197	SAO	3/1/1937	Present
Rutland State Arpt.	43.533	-72.950	239	SAO	8/1/1946	Present
Stewart Field	41.500	-74.100	177	SAO	8/1/1942	Present
Sussex Arpt.	41.200	-74.623	128	SAO	8/28/2000	Present
Tobyhanna Pocono Mtn. A	41.139	-75.223	584	SAO	9/12/1901	Present
Whitefield Mt Washington Reg.	44.368	-71.545	327	SAO	6/1/1971	Present
Hubbard Brook	43.930	-71.720	451	SCAN	M	Present
Lye Brook	43.050	-73.030	742	SCAN	M	Present
Mascoma River	43.780	-72.030	4	SCAN	M	Present
Mount Mansfield	44.530	-72.830	682	SCAN	M	Present

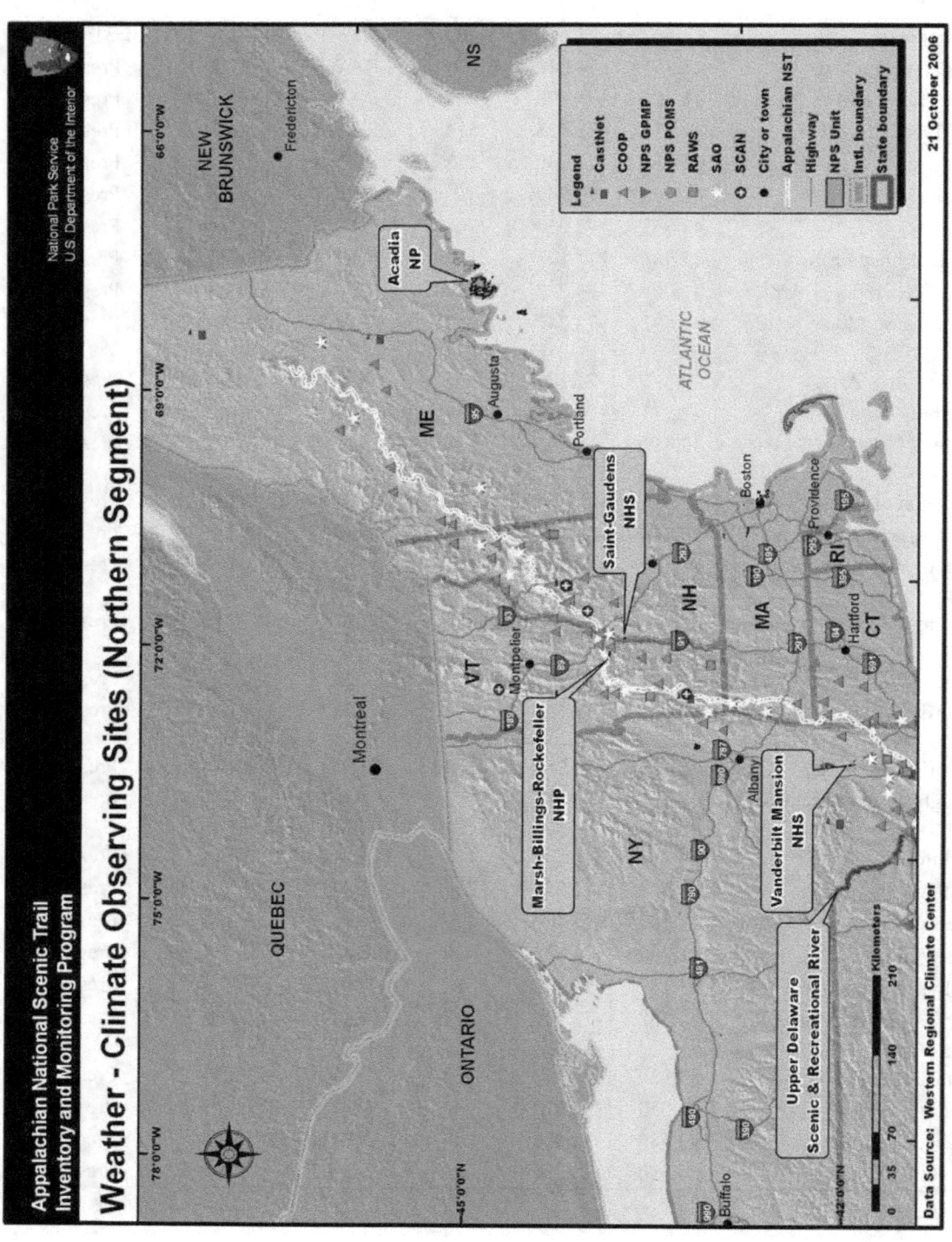

Figure A.3. Station locations for the northern segment of APPA.

64

We identified seven active RAWS stations along the northern segment of APPA (Table A.4). Three of these stations are located within five kilometers of APPA, including "Loch Lomond" in the Delaware Water Gap National Recreation Area, "Hudson Highlands" near West Point, New York, and "Sweezy" near Danby, Vermont (Figure A.3).

In addition to these RAWS stations, there are numerous SAO stations providing near-real-time weather data near and along the northern segment of APPA. Most of these stations are located at local and regional airports. The SAO station with the longest data record is "Tobyhanna Pocono Mtn.," which has been active since 1901 (Table A.4). This station is 20 km northwest of APPA in northeastern Pennsylvania. A COOP station is also located at this site. The SAO station "Greeneville Maine Forestry SVC" is located 10 km northwest of APPA in western Maine and has been active since 1907. One SAO station that is of particular importance to APPA is "Mount Washington," located on the summit of Mt. Washington in New Hampshire (Figure A.3). This station has been active since 1937, has a reliable data record, and is located within a kilometer or so of APPA. A COOP station also operates at this location.

Besides the COOP station on Mt. Washington, there are numerous long-term COOP stations located within 20 km of the northern segment of APPA. In fact, many of the data records go back to the 1800s and early 1900s. Examples of COOP stations that have very long and reliable data records and are located within five kilometers of APPA include "West Point," "Sussex 2 NE," "Port Jervis," "Hanover," and "Berlin."

A.3. Conclusions

Numerous stations, both manual and automated, are available for weather- and climate-monitoring efforts along APPA. There are several key stations located along or very near the trail, including the GPMP site at Clingman's Dome in GRSM, the CASTNet site at Big Meadows in SHEN, and the SAO and COOP stations at the summit of Mt. Washington. Other important stations that provide long-term climate records along APPA include the COOP stations "Waterville 2," near GRSM, and "Hanover," near where APPA crosses the Connecticut River between Vermont and New Hampshire.

65

Appendix B. Glossary

Climate—Complete and entire ensemble of statistical descriptors of temporal and spatial properties comprising the behavior of the atmosphere. These descriptors include means, variances, frequency distributions, autocorrelations, spatial correlations and other patterns of association, temporal lags, and element-to-element relationships. The descriptors have a physical basis in flows and reservoirs of energy and mass. Climate and weather phenomena shade gradually into each other and are ultimately inseparable.

Climate Element—(same as Weather Element) Attribute or property of the state of the atmosphere that is measured, estimated, or derived. Examples of climate elements include temperature, wind speed, wind direction, precipitation amount, precipitation type, relative humidity, dewpoint, solar radiation, snow depth, soil temperature at a given depth, etc. A derived element is a function of other elements (like degree days or number of days with rain) and is not measured directly with a sensor. The terms "parameter" or "variable" are not used to describe elements.

Climate Network—Group of climate stations having a common purpose; the group is often owned and maintained by a single organization.

Climate Station—Station where data are collected to track atmospheric conditions over the long-term. Often, this station operates to additional standards to verify long-term consistency. For these stations, the detailed circumstances surrounding a set of measurements (siting and exposure, instrument changes, etc.) are important.

Data—Measurements specifying the state of the physical environment. Does not include metadata.

Data Inventory—Information about overall data properties for each station within a weather or climate network. A data inventory may include start/stop dates, percentages of available data, breakdowns by climate element, counts of actual data values, counts or fractions of data types, etc. These properties must be determined by actually reading the data and thus require the data to be available, accessible, and in a readable format.

Nor'easter—A strong extratropical low-pressure center that develops along the Atlantic Ocean's Gulf Stream current and moves northeastward along the east coast of the U.S. Strong northeasterly winds along the east coast of the U.S. are common with these storms.

NPS I&M Network—A set of NPS park units grouped by a common theme, typically by natural resource and/or geographic region.

Metadata—Information necessary to interpret environmental data properly, organized as a history or series of snapshots—data about data. Examples include details of measurement processes, station circumstances and exposures, assumptions about the site, network purpose and background, types of observations and sensors, pre-treatment of data, access information, maintenance history and protocols, observational methods, archive locations, owner, and station start/end period.

Quality Assurance—Planned and systematic set of activities to provide adequate confidence that products and services are resulting in credible and correct information. Includes quality control.
Quality Control—Evaluation, assessment, and improvement of imperfect data by utilizing other imperfect data.

Station Inventory—Information about a set of stations obtained from metadata that accompany the network or networks. A station inventory can be compiled from direct and indirect reports prepared by others.

Weather—Instantaneous state of the atmosphere at any given time, mainly with respect to its effects on biological activities. As distinguished from climate, weather consists of the short-term (minutes to days) variations in the atmosphere. Popularly, weather is thought of in terms of temperature, precipitation, humidity, wind, sky condition, visibility, and cloud conditions.

Weather Element (same as Climate Element)—Attribute or property of the state of the atmosphere that is measured, estimated, or derived. Examples of weather elements include temperature, wind speed, wind direction, precipitation amount, precipitation type, relative humidity, dewpoint, solar radiation, snow depth, soil temperature at a given depth, etc. A derived weather element is a function of other elements (like degree days or number of days with rain) and is not measured directly. The terms "parameter" and "variable" are not used to describe weather elements.

Weather Network—Group of weather stations usually owned and maintained by a particular organization and usually for a specific purpose.

Weather Station—Station where collected data are intended for near-real-time use with less need for reference to long-term conditions. In many cases, the detailed circumstances of a set of measurements (siting and exposure, instrument changes, etc.) from weather stations are not as important as for climate stations.

Appendix C. Climate-monitoring principles

Since the late 1990s, frequent references have been made to a set of climate-monitoring principles enunciated in 1996 by Tom Karl, director of the NOAA NCDC in Asheville, North Carolina. These monitoring principles also have been referred to informally as the "Ten Commandments of Climate Monitoring." Both versions are given here. In addition, these principles have been adopted by the Global Climate Observing System (GCOS 2004).

(Compiled by Kelly Redmond, Western Regional Climate Center, Desert Research Institute, August 2000.)

C.1. Full Version (Karl et al. 1996)

C.1.1. Effects on climate records of instrument changes, observing practices, observation locations, sampling rates, etc., must be known before such changes are implemented. This can be ascertained through a period where overlapping measurements from old and new observing systems are collected or sometimes by comparing the old and new observing systems with a reference standard. Site stability for in situ measurements, both in terms of physical location and changes in the nearby environment, also should be a key criterion in site selection. Thus, many synoptic network stations, which are primarily used in weather forecasting but also provide valuable climate data, and dedicated climate stations intended to be operational for extended periods must be subject to this policy.

C.1.2. Processing algorithms and changes in these algorithms must be well documented. Documentation should be carried with the data throughout the data-archiving process.

C.1.3. Knowledge of instrument, station, and/or platform history is essential for interpreting and using the data. Changes in instrument sampling time, local environmental conditions for in situ measurements, and other factors pertinent to interpreting the observations and measurements should be recorded as a mandatory part in the observing routine and be archived with the original data.

C.1.4. In situ and other observations with a long, uninterrupted record should be maintained. Every effort should be applied to protect the data sets that have provided long-term, homogeneous observations. "Long-term" for space-based measurements is measured in decades, but for more conventional measurements, "long-term" may be a century or more. Each element in the observational system should develop a list of prioritized sites or observations based on their contribution to long-term climate monitoring.

C.1.5. Calibration, validation, and maintenance facilities are critical requirements for long-term climatic data sets. Homogeneity in the climate record must be assessed routinely, and corrective action must become part of the archived record.

C.1.6. Where feasible, some level of "low-technology" backup to "high-technology" observing systems should be developed to safeguard against unexpected operational failures.

C.1.7. Regions having insufficient data, variables and regions sensitive to change, and key measurements lacking adequate spatial and temporal resolution should be given the highest priority in designing and implementing new climate-observing systems.

C.1.8. Network designers and instrument engineers must receive long-term climate requirements at the outset of the network design process. This is particularly important because most observing systems have been designed for purposes other than long-term climate monitoring. Instruments must possess adequate accuracy with biases small enough to document climate variations and changes.

C.1.9. Much of the development of new observational capabilities and the evidence supporting the value of these observations stem from research-oriented needs or programs. A lack of stable, long-term commitment to these observations and lack of a clear transition plan from research to operations are two frequent limitations in the development of adequate, long-term monitoring capabilities. Difficulties in securing a long-term commitment must be overcome in order to improve the climate-observing system in a timely manner with minimal interruptions.

C.1.10. Data management systems that facilitate access, use, and interpretation are essential. Freedom of access, low cost, mechanisms that facilitate use (directories, catalogs, browse capabilities, availability of metadata on station histories, algorithm accessibility and documentation, etc.) and quality control should guide data management. International cooperation is critical for successful management of data used to monitor long-term climate change and variability.

C.2. Abbreviated version, "Ten Commandments of Climate Monitoring"

C.2.1. Assess the impact of new climate-observing systems or changes to existing systems before they are implemented.

"Thou shalt properly manage network change." (assess effects of proposed changes)

C.2.2. Require a suitable period where measurement from new and old climate-observing systems will overlap.

"Thou shalt conduct parallel testing." (compare old and replacement systems)

C.2.3. Treat calibration, validation, algorithm-change, and data-homogeneity assessments with the same care as the data.

"Thou shalt collect metadata." (fully document system and operating procedures)

C.2.4. Verify capability for routinely assessing the quality and homogeneity of the data including high-resolution data for extreme events.

"Thou shalt assure data quality and continuity." (assess as part of routine operating procedures)

C.2.5. Integrate assessments like those conducted by the International Panel on Climate Change into global climate-observing priorities.

"Thou shalt anticipate the use of data." (integrated environmental assessment; component in operational plan for system)

C.2.6. Maintain long-term weather and climate stations.

"Thou shalt worship historic significance." (maintain homogeneous data sets from long–term, climate-observing systems)

C.2.7. Place high priority on increasing observations in regions lacking sufficient data and in regions sensitive to change and variability.

"Thou shalt acquire complementary data." (new sites to fill observational gaps)

C.2.8. Provide network operators, designers, and instrument engineers with long-term requirements at the outset of the design and implementation phases for new systems.

"Thou shalt specify requirements for climate observation systems." (application and usage of observational data)

C.2.9. Carefully consider the transition from research-observing system to long-term operation.

"Thou shalt have continuity of purpose." (stable long-term commitments)

C.2.10. Focus on data-management systems that facilitate access, use, and interpretation of weather data and metadata.

"Thou shalt provide access to data and metadata." (readily available weather and climate information)

C.3. Literature Cited

Karl, T. R., V. E. Derr, D. R. Easterling, C. K. Folland, D. J. Hoffman, S. Levitus, N. Nicholls, D. E. Parker, and G. W. Withee. 1996. Critical Issues for Long-Term Climate Monitoring. Pages 55-92 *in* T. R. Karl, editor. Long Term Climate Monitoring by the Global Climate Observing System, Kluwer Publishing.

Global Climate Observing System. 2004. Implementation Plan for the Global Observing System for Climate in Support of the UNFCCC. GCOS-92, WMO/TD No. 1219, World Meteorological Organization, Geneva, Switzerland.

Appendix D. Factors in operating a climate network

D.1. Climate versus Weather
- Climate measurements require _consistency through time._

D.2. Network Purpose
- Anticipated or desired lifetime.
- Breadth of network mission (commitment by needed constituency).
- Dedicated constituency—no network survives without a dedicated constituency.

D.3. Site Identification and Selection
- Spanning gradients in climate or biomes with transects.
- Issues regarding representative spatial scale—site uniformity versus site clustering.
- Alignment with and contribution to network mission.
- Exposure—ability to measure representative quantities.
- Logistics—ability to service station (Always or only in favorable weather?).
- Site redundancy (positive for quality control, negative for extra resources).
- Power—is AC needed?
- Site security—is protection from vandalism needed?
- Permitting often a major impediment and usually underestimated.

D.4. Station Hardware
- Survival—weather is the main cause of lost weather/climate data.
- Robustness of sensors—ability to measure and record in any condition.
- Quality—distrusted records are worthless and a waste of time and money.
  - High quality—will cost up front but pays off later.
  - Low quality—may provide a lower start-up cost but will cost more later (low cost can be expensive).
- Redundancy—backup if sensors malfunction.
- Ice and snow—measurements are much more difficult than rain measurements.
- Severe environments (expense is about two–three times greater than for stations in more benign settings).

D.5. Communications
- Reliability—live data have a much larger constituency.
- One-way or two-way.
  - Retrieval of missed transmissions.
  - Ability to reprogram data logger remotely.
  - Remote troubleshooting abilities.
  - Continuing versus one-time costs.
- Back-up procedures to prevent data loss during communication outages.
- Live communications increase problems but also increase value.

D.6. Maintenance
- Main reason why networks fail (and most networks do eventually fail!).

- <u>Key</u> issue with nearly every network.
- Who will perform maintenance?
- Degree of commitment and motivation to contribute.
- Periodic? On-demand as needed? Preventive?
- Equipment change-out schedules and upgrades for sensors and software.
- Automated stations require <u>skilled</u> and <u>experienced</u> labor.
- Calibration—sensors often drift (climate).
- Site maintenance essential (constant vegetation, surface conditions, nearby influences).
- Typical automated station will cost about $2K per year to maintain.
- Documentation—photos, notes, visits, changes, essential for posterity.
- Planning for equipment life cycle and technological advances.

D.7. Maintaining Programmatic Continuity and Corporate Knowledge
- Long-term vision and commitment needed.
- Institutionalizing versus personalizing—developing appropriate dependencies.

D.8. Data Flow
- Centralized ingest?
- Centralized access to data and data products?
- Local version available?
- Contract out work or do it yourself?
- Quality control of data.
- Archival.
- Metadata—historic information, not a snapshot. Every station should collect metadata.
- Post-collection processing, multiple data-ingestion paths.

D.9. Products
- Most basic product consists of the data values.
- Summaries.
- Write own applications or leverage existing mechanisms?

D.10. Funding
- Prototype approaches as proof of concept.
- Linking and leveraging essential.
- Constituencies—every network <u>needs</u> a constituency.
- Bridging to practical and operational communities? Live data needed.
- Bridging to counterpart research efforts and initiatives—funding source.
- Creativity, resourcefulness, and persistence usually are essential to success.

D.11. Final Comments
- Deployment is by far the easiest part in operating a network.
- Maintenance is the main issue.
- Best analogy: Operating a network is like raising a child; it requires constant attention.

Source: Western Regional Climate Center (WRCC)

Appendix E. General design considerations for weather/climate-monitoring programs

The process for designing a climate-monitoring program benefits from anticipating design and protocol issues discussed here. Much of this material is been excerpted from a report addressing the Channel Islands National Park (Redmond and McCurdy 2005), where an example is found illustrating how these factors can be applied to a specific setting. Many national park units possess some climate or meteorology feature that sets them apart from more familiar or "standard" settings.

E.1. Introduction

There are several criteria that must be used in deciding to deploy new stations and where these new stations should be sited.

- Where are existing stations located?
- Where have data been gathered in the past (discontinued locations)?
- Where would a new station fill a knowledge gap about basic, long-term climatic averages for an area of interest?
- Where would a new station fill a knowledge gap about how climate behaves over time?
- As a special case for behavior over time, what locations might be expected to show a more sensitive response to climate change?
- How do answers to the preceding questions depend on the climate element? Are answers the same for precipitation, temperature, wind, snowfall, humidity, etc.?
- What role should manual measurements play? How should manual measurements interface with automated measurements?
- Are there special technical or management issues, either present or anticipated in the next 5–15 years, requiring added climate information?
- What unique information is provided in addition to information from existing sites? "Redundancy is bad."
- What nearby information is available to estimate missing observations because observing systems always experience gaps and lose data? "Redundancy is good."
- How would logistics and maintenance affect these decisions?

In relation to the preceding questions, there are several topics that should be considered. The following topics are not listed in a particular order.

E.1.1. Network Purpose

Humans seem to have an almost reflexive need to measure temperature and precipitation, along with other climate elements. These reasons span a broad range from utilitarian to curiosity-driven. Although there are well-known recurrent patterns of need and data use, new uses are always appearing. The number of uses ranges in the thousands. Attempts have been made to categorize such uses (see NRC, 1998; NRC, 2001). Because climate measurements are accumulated over a long time, they should be treated as multi-purpose and should be undertaken in a manner that serves the widest possible applications. Some applications remain constant, while others rise and fall in importance. An insistent issue today may subside, while the next pressing issue of tomorrow barely may be anticipated. The notion that humans might affect the climate of the entire Earth was nearly unimaginable when the national USDA (later NOAA) cooperative weather network began in the late 1800s. Abundant experience has shown, however, that there always will be a demand for a history record of climate measurements and their properties. Experience also shows that there is an expectation that climate measurements will be taken and made available to the general public.

An exhaustive list of uses for data would fill many pages and still be incomplete. In broad terms, however, there are needs to document environmental conditions that disrupt or otherwise affect park operations (e.g., storms and droughts). Design and construction standards are determined by climatological event frequencies that exceed certain thresholds. Climate is a determinant that sometimes attracts and sometimes discourages visitors. Climate may play a large part in the park experience (e.g., Death Valley and heat are nearly synonymous). Some park units are large enough to encompass spatial or elevation diversity in climate, and the sequence of events can vary considerably inside or close to park boundaries. That is, temporal trends and statistics may not be the same everywhere, and this spatial structure should be sampled. The granularity of this structure depends on the presence of topography or large climate gradients or both, such as that found along the U.S. West Coast in summer with the rapid transition from the marine layer to the hot interior.

Plant and animal communities and entire ecosystems react to every nuance in the physical environment. No aspect of weather and climate goes undetected in the natural world. Wilson (1998) proposed "an informal rule of biological evolution" that applies here: "If an organic sensor can be imagined that is capable of detecting any particular environmental signal, a species exists somewhere that possesses this sensor." Every weather and climate event, whether dull or extraordinary to humans, matters to some organism. Dramatic events and creeping incremental change both have consequences to living systems. Extreme events or disturbances can "reset the clock" or "shake up the system" and lead to reverberations that last for years to centuries or longer. Slow change can carry complex nonlinear systems (e.g., any living assemblage) into states where chaotic transitions and new behavior occur. These changes are seldom predictable, typically are observed after the fact, and understood only in retrospect. Climate changes may not be exciting, but as a well-known atmospheric scientist, Mike Wallace, from the University of Washington once noted, "subtle does not mean unimportant."

Thus, individuals who observe the climate should be able to record observations accurately and depict both rapid and slow changes. In particular, an array of artificial influences easily can confound detection of slow changes. The record as provided can contain both real climate variability (that took place in the atmosphere) and fake climate variability (that arose directly from the way atmospheric changes were observed and recorded). As an example, trees growing near a climate station with an excellent anemometer will make it appear that the wind gradually slowed down over many years. Great care must be taken to protect against sources of fake climate variability on the longer-time scales of years to decades. Processes leading to the observed climate are not stationary; rather these processes draw from probability distributions that vary with time. For this reason, climatic time series do not exhibit statistical stationarity. The implications are manifold. There are no true climatic "normals" to which climate inevitably must return. Rather, there are broad ranges of climatic conditions. Climate does not demonstrate exact repetition but instead continual fluctuation and sometimes approximate repetition. In addition, there is always new behavior waiting to occur. Consequently, the business of climate monitoring is never finished, and there is no point where we can state confidently that "enough" is known.

E.1.2. Robustness

The most frequent cause for loss of weather data is the weather itself, the very thing we wish to record. The design of climate and weather observing programs should consider the meteorological equivalent of "peaking power" employed by utilities. Because environmental disturbances have significant effects on ecologic systems, sensors, data loggers, and communications networks should be able to function during the most severe conditions that realistically can be anticipated over the next 50–100 years. Systems designed in this manner are less likely to fail under more ordinary conditions, as well as more likely to transmit continuous, quality data for both tranquil and active periods.

E.1.3. Weather versus Climate

For "weather" measurements, pertaining to what is approximately happening here and now, small moves and changes in exposure are not as critical. For "climate" measurements, where values from different points in time are compared, siting and exposure are critical factors, and it is vitally important that the observing circumstances remain essentially unchanged over the duration of the station record.

Station moves can affect different elements to differing degrees. Even small moves of several meters, especially vertically, can affect temperature records. Hills and knolls act differently from the bottoms of small swales, pockets, or drainage channels (Geiger et al. 2003; Whiteman 2000). Precipitation is probably less subject to change with moves of 50–100 m than other elements (that is, precipitation has less intrinsic variation in small spaces) except if wind flow over the gauge is affected.

E.1.4. Physical Setting

Siting and exposure, and their continuity and consistency through time, significantly influence the climate records produced by a station. These two terms have overlapping connotations. We use the term "siting" in a more general sense, reserving the term "exposure" generally for the particular circumstances affecting the ability of an instrument to record measurements that are representative of the desired spatial or temporal scale.

E.1.5. Measurement Intervals

Climatic processes occur continuously in time, but our measurement systems usually record in discrete chunks of time: for example, seconds, hours, or days. These measurements often are referred to as "systematic" measurements. Interval averages may hide active or interesting periods of highly intense activity. Alternatively, some systems record "events" when a certain threshold of activity is exceeded (examples: another millimeter of precipitation has fallen, another kilometer of wind has moved past, the temperature has changed by a degree, a gust higher than 9.9 m/s has been measured). When this occurs, measurements from all sensors are reported. These measurements are known as "breakpoint" data. In relatively unchanging conditions (long calm periods or rainless weeks, for example), event recorders should send a signal that they are still "alive and well." If systematic recorders are programmed to note and periodically report the highest, lowest, and mean value within each time interval, the likelihood is reduced that interesting behavior will be glossed over or lost. With the capacity of modern data loggers, it is recommended to record and report extremes within the basic time increment (e.g., hourly or 10 minutes). This approach also assists quality-control procedures.

There is usually a trade-off between data volume and time increment, and most automated systems now are set to record approximately hourly. A number of field stations maintained by WRCC are programmed to record in 5- or 10-minute increments, which are then used to construct an hourly value. However, this approach produces 6–12 times as much data as hourly data. These systems typically do not record details of events at sub-interval time scales, but they easily can record peak values, or counts of threshold exceedance, within the time intervals.

Thus, for each time interval at an automated station, we recommend that several kinds of information—mean or sum, extreme maximum and minimum, and sometimes standard deviation—be recorded. These measurements are useful for quality control and other purposes. Modern data loggers and office computers have quite high capacity. Diagnostic information indicating the state of solar chargers or battery voltages and their extremes is of great value. This topic will be discussed in greater detail in a succeeding section.

Automation also has made possible adaptive or intelligent monitoring techniques where systems vary the recording rate based on detection of the behavior of interest by the software. For example, sub-interval behaviors of interest (e.g., a 5-minute extreme downpour with high-erosive capability hidden by an innocuous hourly total) can be detected when a breakpoint is exceeded, whereas this event might otherwise be concealed if it occurred between scheduled measurement intervals (e.g. hourly sampling). Most users prefer measurements that are systematic in time because they are much easier to summarize and manipulate.

For breakpoint data produced by event reporters, there also is a need to send periodically a signal that the station is still functioning, even though there is nothing more to report. "No report" does not necessarily mean "no data," and it is important to distinguish between the actual observation that was recorded and the content of that observation (e.g., an observation of "0.00" is not the same as "no observation").

E.1.6. Mixed Time Scales
There are times when we may wish to combine information from radically different scales. For example, over the past 100 years we may want to know how the frequency of 5-minute precipitation peaks has varied or how the frequency of peak 1-second wind gusts have varied. We may also want to know over this time if nearby vegetation gradually has grown up to increasingly block the wind or to slowly improve precipitation catch. Answers to these questions require knowledge over a wide range of time scales.

E.1.7. Elements
For manual measurements, the typical elements recorded included temperature extremes, precipitation, and snowfall/snow depth. However, automated measurements typically include temperature, precipitation, humidity, wind speed and direction, and solar radiation. An exception to this exists in very windy locations where precipitation is difficult to measure accurately. Automated measurements of snow are improving, but manual measurements are still preferable,

as long as shielding is present. Automated measurement of frozen precipitation presents numerous challenges that have not been resolved fully, and the best gauges are quite expensive ($3000–8000). Soil temperatures may also be measured. Soil moisture is extremely useful, but measurements are not made at many sites. In addition, care must be taken in the installation and maintenance of instruments used in measuring soil moisture. Soil properties vary tremendously in short distances as well, and it is often very difficult ("impossible") to accurately document these variations (without digging up all the soil!). In cooler climates, ultrasonic sensors that detect snow depth are becoming commonplace.

E.1.8. Wind Standards

Wind varies the most in the shortest distance, since it always decreases to zero near the ground and increases rapidly (approximately logarithmically) with height near the ground. Changes in anemometer height obviously will affect distribution of wind speed as will changes in vegetation, obstructions such as buildings, etc. Everything else being equal, a site that has a 3-m (10-ft) mast will generally be less windy than a site that has a 6-m (20-ft) or 10-m (33-ft) mast. Historically, many U.S. airports (FAA and NWS) and most current RAWS sites have used a standard 6-m (20-ft) mast for wind measurements. Some NPS RAWS sites utilize shorter masts. Over the last decade, as Automated Surface Observing Systems (ASOSs, mostly NWS) and Automated Weather Observing Systems (AWOSs, mostly FAA) have been deployed at most airports, wind masts have been raised to 8 or 10 m (26 or 33 ft), depending on airplane clearance. The World Meteorological Organization recommends 10 m as the height for wind measurements (WMO 1983; 2005), and more groups are migrating slowly to this standard. The American Association of State Climatologists (AASC 1985) have recommended that wind be measured at 3 m, a standard geared more for agricultural applications than for general purpose uses where higher levels usually are preferred. Different anemometers have different starting thresholds; therefore, areas that are measured by instruments with higher starting thresholds and/or frequently experience very light winds may not produce wind measurements which, in turn, would affect long-term mean estimates of wind speed. For both sustained winds (averages over a short interval of 2–60 minutes) and especially for gusts, the duration of the sampling interval makes considerable difference. For the same wind history, 1–second gusts are higher than gusts averaging 3 seconds, which in turn are greater than 5-second averages, so that the same sequence would be described with different numbers (all three systems and more are in use). Changes in the averaging procedure, or in height or exposure, can lead to "false" or "fake" climate change with no change in actual climate. Changes in any of these should be noted in the metadata.

E.1.9. Wind Nomenclature

Wind is a vector quantity having a direction and a speed. Directions can be two- or three-dimensional; they will be three-dimensional if the vertical component is important. In all common uses, winds always are denoted by the direction they blow *from* (north wind or southerly breeze). This convention exists because wind often brings weather, and thus our attention is focused upstream. However, this approach contrasts with the way ocean currents are viewed. Ocean currents usually are denoted by the direction they are moving *towards* (eastward current moves from west to east). In specialized applications (such as in atmospheric modeling), wind velocity vectors point in the direction that the wind is blowing. Thus, a southwesterly wind (from the southwest) has both northward and eastward (to the north and to the east) components.

Except near mountains, wind cannot blow up or down near the ground, so the vertical component of wind often is approximated as zero, and the horizontal component is emphasized.

E.1.10. Frozen Precipitation

Frozen precipitation is more difficult to measure than liquid precipitation, especially with automated techniques. Goodison et al. (1998), Sevruk and Harmon (1984), Yang et al. (1998, 2001) provide many of the reasons to explain this. The importance of frozen precipitation varies greatly from one setting to another. This subject was discussed in greater detail in a related inventory and monitoring report for the Alaska park units (Redmond et al. 2005).

In climates that receive frozen precipitation, a decision must be made whether or not to try to record such events accurately. This usually means that the precipitation must be turned into liquid either by falling into an antifreeze fluid solution that is then weighed or by heating the precipitation enough to melt and fall through a measuring mechanism such as a nearly-balanced tipping bucket. Accurate measurements from the first approach require expensive gauges; tipping buckets can achieve this resolution readily but are more apt to lose some or all precipitation. Improvements have been made to the heating mechanism on the NWS tipping-bucket gauge used for the ASOS to correct its numerous deficiencies making it less problematic; however, this gauge is not inexpensive. A heat supply needed to melt frozen precipitation usually requires more energy than renewable energy (solar panels or wind recharging) can provide thus AC power is needed. The availability of AC power is severely limited in many cold or remote U. S. settings. Furthermore, periods of frozen precipitation or rime often provide less-than-optimal recharging conditions with heavy clouds, short days, low-solar-elevation angles and more horizon blocking, and cold temperatures causing additional drain on the battery.

E.1.11. Save or Lose

A second consideration with precipitation is determining if the measurement should be saved (as in weighing systems) or lost (as in tipping-bucket systems). With tipping buckets, after the water has passed through the tipping mechanism, it usually just drops to the ground. Thus, there is no checksum to ensure that the sum of all the tips adds up to what has been saved in a reservoir at some location. By contrast, weighing gauges continually accumulate precipitation until the reservoir is emptied, the reported value is the total reservoir content (for example, the height of the liquid column in a tube), and the incremental precipitation is the difference in depth between two known times. These weighing gauges do not always have the same fine resolution. Some gauges only record to the nearest centimeter, which is usually acceptable for hydrology but not necessarily for other needs. (For reference, a millimeter of precipitation can get a person in street clothes quite wet.) This is how the NRCS/USDA SNOTEL system works in climates that measure up to 3000 cm of snow in a winter. (See http://www.wcc.nrcs.usda.gov/publications for publications or http://www.wcc.nrcs.usda.gov/factpub/aib536.html for a specific description.) No precipitation is lost this way. A thin layer of oil is used to suppress evaporation, and anti-freeze ensures that frozen precipitation melts. When initially recharged, the sum of the oil and starting antifreeze solution is treated as the zero point. The anti-freeze usually is not sufficiently environmentally friendly to discharge to the ground and thus must be hauled into the area and then back out. Other weighing gauges are capable of measuring to the 0.25-mm (0.01-in.) resolution but do not have as much capacity and must be emptied more often. Day/night and storm-related thermal expansion and contraction and sometimes wind shaking can cause fluid pressure from accumulated totals to go up and down in SNOTEL gauges by small increments (commonly 0.3-3 cm, or 0.01–0.10 ft) leading to "negative precipitation" followed by similarly non-real light precipitation when, in fact, no change took place in the amount of accumulated precipitation.

E.1.12. Time

Time should always be in local standard time (LST), and daylight savings time (DST) should never be used under any circumstances with automated equipment and timers. Using DST leads to one duplicate hour, one missing hour, and a season of displaced values, as well as needless confusion and a data-management nightmare. Absolute time, such as Greenwich Mean Time (GMT) or Coordinated Universal Time (UTC), also can be used because these formats are unambiguously translatable. Since measurements only provide information about what already *has* occurred or *is* occurring and not what *will* occur, they should always be assigned to the *ending time* of the associated interval with hour 24 marking the end of the last hour of the day. In this system, midnight always represents the end of the day, not the start. To demonstrate the importance of this differentiation, we have encountered situations where police officers seeking corroborating weather data could not recall whether the time on their crime report from a year ago was the starting midnight or the ending midnight! Station positions should be known to within a few meters, easily accomplished with GPS, so that time zones and solar angles can be determined accurately.

E.1.13. Automated versus Manual

Most of this report has addressed automated measurements. Historically, most measurements are manual and typically collected once a day. In many cases, manual measurements continue because of habit, usefulness, and desire for continuity over time. Manual measurements are extremely useful and when possible should be encouraged. However, automated measurements are becoming more common. For either, it is important to record time in a logically consistent manner.

It should not be automatically assumed that newer data and measurements are "better" than older data or that manual data are "worse" than automated data. Older or simpler manual measurements are often of very high quality even if they sometimes are not in the most convenient digital format.

There is widespread desire to use automated systems to reduce human involvement. This is admirable and understandable, but every automated weather/climate station or network requires significant human attention and maintenance. A telling example concerns the Oklahoma Mesonet (see Brock et al. 1995, and bibliography at http://www.mesonet.ou.edu), a network of about 115 high–quality, automated meteorological stations spread over Oklahoma, where about 80 percent of the annual ($2–3M) budget is nonetheless allocated to humans with only about 20 percent allocated to equipment.

E.1.14. Manual Conventions

Manual measurements typically are made once a day. Elements usually consist of maximum and minimum temperature, temperature at observation time, precipitation, snowfall, snow depth, and sometimes evaporation, wind, or other information. Since it is not actually known when extremes occurred, the only logical approach, and the nationwide convention, is to ascribe the entire measurement to the time-interval date and to enter it on the form in that way. For morning observers (for example, 8 am to 8 am), this means that the maximum temperature written for today often is from yesterday afternoon and sometimes the minimum temperature for the 24-hr period actually occurred yesterday morning. However, this is understood and expected. It is often a surprise to observers to see how many maximum temperatures do not occur in the afternoon and how many minimum temperatures do not occur in the predawn hours. This is especially true in environments that are colder, higher, northerly, cloudy, mountainous, or coastal. As long as this convention is strictly followed every day, it has been shown that truly excellent climate records can result (Redmond 1992). Manual observers should reset equipment only one time per day at the official observing time. Making more than one measurement a day is discouraged strongly; this practice results in a hybrid record that is too difficult to interpret. The only exception is for total daily snowfall. New snowfall can be measured up to four times per day with no observations closer than six hours. It is well known that more frequent measurement of snow increases the annual total because compaction is a continuous process.

Two main purposes for climate observations are to establish the long-term averages for given locations and to track variations in climate. Broadly speaking, these purposes address topics of absolute and relative climate behavior. Once absolute behavior has been "established" (a task that is never finished because long-term averages continue to vary in time)—temporal variability quickly becomes the item of most interest.

E.2. Representativeness
Having discussed important factors to consider when new sites are installed, we now turn our attention to site "representativeness." In popular usage, we often encounter the notion that a site is "representative" of another site if it receives the same annual precipitation or records the same annual temperature or if some other element-specific, long-term average has a similar value. This notion of representativeness has a certain limited validity, but there are other aspects of this idea that need to be considered.

A climate monitoring site also can be said to be representative if climate records from that site show sufficiently strong temporal correlations with a large number of locations over a sufficiently large area. If station A receives 20 cm a year and station B receives 200 cm a year, these climates obviously receive quite differing amounts of precipitation. However, if their monthly, seasonal, or annual correlations are high (for example, 0.80 or higher for a particular time scale), one site can be used as a surrogate for estimating values at the other if measurements for a particular month, season, or year are missing. That is, a wet or dry month at one station is also a wet or dry month (relative to its own mean) at the comparison station. Note that high correlations on one time scale do not imply automatically that high correlations will occur on other time scales.

Likewise, two stations having similar mean climates (for example, similar annual precipitation) might not co-vary in close synchrony (for example, coastal versus interior). This may be considered a matter of climate "affiliation" for a particular location.

Thus, the representativeness of a site can refer either to the basic climatic averages for a given duration (or time window within the annual cycle) or to the extent that the site co-varies in time with respect to all surrounding locations. One site can be representative of another in the first sense but not the second, or vice versa, or neither, or both—all combinations are possible. If two sites are perfectly correlated then, in a sense, they are "redundant." However, redundancy has value because all sites will experience missing data especially with automated equipment in rugged environments and harsh climates where outages and other problems nearly can be guaranteed. In many cases, those outages are caused by the weather, particularly by unusual weather and the very conditions we most wish to know about. Methods for filling in those values will require proxy information from this or other nearby networks. Thus, redundancy is a virtue rather than a vice.

In general, the cooperative stations managed by the NWS have produced much longer records than automated stations like RAWS or SNOTEL stations. The RAWS stations often have problems with precipitation, especially in winter, or with missing data, so that low correlations may be data problems rather than climatic dissimilarity. The RAWS records also are relatively short, so correlations should be interpreted with care. In performing and interpreting such analyses, however, we must remember that there are physical climate reasons and observational reasons why stations within a short distance (even a few tens or hundreds of meters) may not correlate well.

E.2.1. Temporal Behavior

It is possible that high correlations will occur between station pairs during certain portions of the year (i.e., January) but low correlations may occur during other portions of the year (e.g., September or October). The relative contributions of these seasons to the annual total (for precipitation) or average (for temperature) and the correlations for each month are both factors in the correlation of an aggregated time window of longer duration that encompasses those seasons (e.g., one of the year definitions such as calendar year or water year). A complete and careful evaluation ideally would include such a correlation analysis but requires more resources and data. Note that it also is possible and frequently is observed that temperatures are highly correlated while precipitation is not or vice versa, and these relations can change according to the time of year. If two stations are well correlated for all climate elements for all portions of the year, then they can be considered redundant.

With scarce resources, the initial strategy should be to try to identify locations that do not correlate particularly well, so that each new site measures something new that cannot be guessed easily from the behavior of surrounding sites. (An important caveat here is that lack of such correlation could be a result of physical climate behavior and not a result of faults with the actual measuring process; i.e., by unrepresentative or simply poor-quality data. Unfortunately, we seldom have perfect climate data.) As additional sites are added, we usually wish for some combination of unique and redundant sites to meet what amounts to essentially orthogonal constraints: new information and more reliably-furnished information.

A common consideration is whether to observe on a ridge or in a valley, given the resources to place a single station within a particular area of a few square kilometers. Ridge and valley stations will correlate very well for temperatures when lapse conditions prevail, particularly summer daytime temperatures. In summer at night or winter at daylight, the picture will be more mixed and correlations will be lower. In winter at night when inversions are common and even the rule, correlations may be zero or even negative and perhaps even more divergent as the two sites are on opposite sides of the inversion. If we had the luxury of locating stations everywhere, we would find that ridge tops generally correlate very well with other ridge tops and similarly valleys with other valleys, but ridge tops correlate well with valleys only under certain circumstances. Beyond this, valleys and ridges having similar orientations usually will correlate better with each other than those with perpendicular orientations, depending on their orientation with respect to large-scale wind flow and solar angles.

Unfortunately, we do not have stations everywhere, so we are forced to use the few comparisons that we have and include a large dose of intelligent reasoning, using what we have observed elsewhere. In performing and interpreting such analyses, we must remember that there are physical climatic reasons and observational reasons why stations within a short distance (even a few tens or hundreds of meters) may not correlate well.

Examples of correlation analyses include those for the Channel Islands and for southwest Alaska, which can be found in Redmond and McCurdy (2005) and Redmond et al. (2005). These examples illustrate what can be learned from correlation analyses. Spatial correlations generally vary by time of year. Thus, results should be displayed in the form of annual correlation cycles—for monthly mean temperature and monthly total precipitation and perhaps other climate elements like wind or humidity—between station pairs selected for climatic setting and data availability and quality.

In general, the COOP stations managed by the NWS have produced much longer records than have automated stations like RAWS or SNOTEL stations. Furthermore, RAWS stations often have problems with precipitation, especially in winter or with missing data, so that low correlations may be data problems rather than climate dissimilarity. The RAWS records are much shorter, so correlations should be interpreted with care, but these stations are more likely to be in places of interest for remote or under-sampled regions.

E.2.2. Spatial Behavior

A number of techniques exist to interpolate from isolated point values to a spatial domain. For example, a common technique is simple inverse distance weighting. Critical to the success of the simplest of such techniques is that some other property of the spatial domain, one that is influential for the mapped element, does not vary significantly. Topography greatly influences precipitation, temperature, wind, humidity, and most other meteorological elements. Thus, this criterion clearly is not met in any region having extreme topographic diversity. In such circumstances, simple Cartesian distance may have little to do with how rapidly correlation deteriorates from one site to the next, and in fact, the correlations can decrease readily from a mountain to a valley and then increase again on the next mountain. Such structure in the fields of spatial correlation is not seen in the relatively (statistically) well-behaved flat areas like those in the eastern United States.

To account for dominating effects such as topography and inland–coastal differences that exist in certain regions, some kind of additional knowledge must be brought to bear to produce meaningful, physically plausible, and observationally based interpolations. Historically, this has proven to be an extremely difficult problem, especially to perform objective and repeatable analyses. An analysis performed for southwest Alaska (Redmond et al. 2005) concluded that the PRISM (Parameter Regression on Independent Slopes Model) maps (Daly et al. 1994, 2002; Gibson et al., 2002; Doggett et al., 2004) were probably the best available. An analysis by Simpson et al. (2005) further discussed many issues in the mapping of Alaska's climate and resulted in the same conclusion about PRISM.

E.2.3. Climate-Change Detection
Although general purpose climate stations should be situated to address all aspects of climate variability, it is desirable that they also be in locations that are more sensitive to climate change from natural or anthropogenic influences should it begin to occur. The question here is how well we know such sensitivities. The polar regions and especially the North Pole are generally regarded as being more sensitive to changes in radiative forcing of climate because of positive feedbacks. The climate-change issue is quite complex because it encompasses more than just greenhouse gasses.

Sites that are in locations or climates particularly vulnerable to climate change should be favored. How this vulnerability is determined is a considerably challenging research issue. Candidate locations or situations are those that lie on the border between two major biomes or just inside the edge of one or the other. In these cases, a slight movement of the boundary in anticipated direction (toward "warmer," for example) would be much easier to detect as the boundary moves past the site and a different set of biota begin to be established. Such a vegetative or ecologic response would be more visible and would take less time to establish as a real change than would a smaller change in the center of the distribution range of a marker or key species.

E.2.4. Element-Specific Differences
The various climate elements (temperature, precipitation, cloudiness, snowfall, humidity, wind speed and direction, solar radiation) do not vary through time in the same sequence or manner nor should they necessarily be expected to vary in this manner. The spatial patterns of variability should not be expected to be the same for all elements. These patterns also should not be expected to be similar for all months or seasons. The suitability of individual sites for measurement also varies from one element to another. A site that has a favorable exposure for temperature or wind may not have a favorable exposure for precipitation or snowfall. A site that experiences proper air movement may be situated in a topographic channel, such as a river valley or a pass, which restricts the range of wind directions and affects the distribution of speed-direction categories.

E.2.5. Logistics and Practical Factors
Even with the most advanced scientific rationale, sites in some remote or climatically challenging settings may not be suitable because of the difficulty in servicing and maintaining equipment. Contributing to these challenges are scheduling difficulties, animal behavior, snow burial, icing, snow behavior, access and logistical problems, and the weather itself. Remote and elevated sites usually require far more attention and expense than a rain-dominated, easily accessible valley location.

For climate purposes, station exposure and the local environment should be maintained in their original state (vegetation especially), so that changes seen are the result of regional climate variations and not of trees growing up, bushes crowding a site, surface albedo changing, fire clearing, etc. Repeat photography has shown many examples of slow environmental change in the vicinity of a station in rather short time frames (5–20 years), and this technique should be employed routinely and frequently at all locations. In the end, logistics, maintenance, and other practical factors almost always determine the success of weather- and climate-monitoring activities.

E.2.6. Personnel Factors

Many past experiences (almost exclusively negative) strongly support the necessity to place primary responsibility for station deployment and maintenance in the hands of seasoned, highly qualified, trained, and meticulously careful personnel, the more experienced the better. Over time, even in "benign" climates but especially where harsher conditions prevail, every conceivable problem will occur and both the usual and unusual should be anticipated: weather, animals, plants, salt, sensor and communication failure, windblown debris, corrosion, power failures, vibrations, avalanches, snow loading and creep, corruption of the data logger program, etc. An ability to anticipate and forestall such problems, a knack for innovation and improvisation, knowledge of electronics, practical and organizational skills, and presence of mind to bring the various small but vital parts, spares, tools, and diagnostic troubleshooting equipment are highly valued qualities. Especially when logistics are so expensive, a premium should be placed on using experienced personnel, since the slightest and seemingly most minor mistake can render a station useless or, even worse, uncertain. Exclusive reliance on individuals without this background can be costly and almost always will result eventually in unnecessary loss of data. Skilled labor and an apprenticeship system to develop new skilled labor will greatly reduce (but not eliminate) the types of problems that can occur in operating a climate network.

E.3. Site Selection

In addition to considerations identified previously in this appendix, various factors need to be considered in selecting sites for new or augmented instrumentation.

E.3.1. Equipment and Exposure Factors

E.3.1.1. Measurement Suite: All sites should measure temperature, humidity, wind, solar radiation, and snow depth. Precipitation measurements are more difficult but probably should be attempted with the understanding that winter measurements may be of limited or no value unless an all-weather gauge has been installed. Even if an all-weather gauge has been installed, it is desirable to have a second gauge present that operates on a different principle–for example, a fluid-based system like those used in the SNOTEL stations in tandem with a higher–resolution, tipping bucket gauge for summertime. Without heating, a tipping bucket gauge usually is of use only when temperatures are above freezing and when temperatures have not been below freezing for some time, so that accumulated ice and snow is not melting and being recorded as present precipitation. Gauge undercatch is a significant issue in snowy climates, so shielding should be considered for all gauges designed to work over the winter months. It is very important to note the presence or absence of shielding, the type of shielding, and the dates of installation or removal of the shielding.

E.3.1.2. Overall Exposure: The ideal, general all-purpose site has gentle slopes, is open to the sun and the wind, has a natural vegetative cover, avoids strong local (less than 200 m) influences, and represents a reasonable compromise among all climate elements. The best temperature sites are not the best precipitation sites, and the same is true for other elements. Steep topography in the immediate vicinity should be avoided unless settings where precipitation is affected by steep topography are being deliberately sought or a mountaintop or ridgeline is the desired location. The potential for disturbance should be considered: fire and flood risk, earth movement, wind-borne debris, volcanic deposits or lahars, vandalism, animal tampering, and general human encroachment are all factors.

E.3.1.3. Elevation: Mountain climates do not vary in time in exactly the same manner as adjoining valley climates. This concept is emphasized when temperature inversions are present to a greater degree and during precipitation when winds rise up the slopes at the same angle. There is considerable concern that mountain climates will be (or already are) changing and perhaps changing differently than lowland climates, which has direct and indirect consequences for plant and animal life in the more extreme zones. Elevations of special significance are those that are near the mean rain/snow line for winter, near the tree line, and near the mean annual freezing level (all of these may not be quite the same). Because the lapse rates in wet climates often are nearly moist-adiabatic during the main precipitation seasons, measurements at one elevation may be extrapolated to nearby elevations. In drier climates and in the winter, temperature and to a lesser extent wind will show various elevation profiles.

E.3.1.4. Transects: The concept of observing transects that span climatic gradients is sound. This is not always straightforward in topographically uneven terrain, but these transects could still be arranged by setting up station(s) along the coast; in or near passes atop the main coastal interior drainage divide; and inland at one, two, or three distances into the interior lowlands. Transects need not—and because of topographic constraints probably cannot—be straight lines, but the closer that a line can be approximated the better. The main point is to systematically sample the key points of a behavioral transition without deviating too radically from linearity.

E.3.1.5. Other Topographic Considerations: There are various considerations with respect to local topography. Local topography can influence wind (channeling, upslope/downslope, etc.), precipitation (orographic enhancement, downslope evaporation, catch efficiency, etc.), and temperature (frost pockets, hilltops, aspect, mixing or decoupling from the overlying atmosphere, bowls, radiative effects, etc.), to different degrees at differing scales. In general, for measurements to represent an area, it is better to avoid these local effects to the extent that they can be identified before station deployment (once deployed, it is desirable not to move a station). The primary purpose of a climate-monitoring network should be to serve as an infrastructure in the form of a set of benchmark stations for comparing other stations. Sometimes, however, it is exactly these local phenomena that we want to capture. Living organisms, especially plants, are affected by their immediate environment, whether it is representative of a larger setting or not. Specific measurements of limited scope and duration made for these purposes then can be tied to the main benchmarks. This experience is useful also in determining the complexity needed in the benchmark monitoring process in order to capture particular phenomena at particular space and time scales.

Sites that drain (cold air) well generally are better than sites that allow cold air to pool. Slightly sloped areas (1 degree is fine) or small benches from tens to hundreds of meters above streams are often favorable locations. Furthermore, these sites often tend to be out of the path of hazards (like floods) and to have rocky outcroppings where controlling vegetation will not be a major concern. Benches or wide spots on the rise between two forks of a river system are often the only flat areas and sometimes jut out to give greater exposure to winds from more directions.

E.3.1.6. Prior History: The starting point in designing a program is to determine what kinds of observations have been collected over time, by whom, in what manner, and if these observation are continuing to the present time. It also may be of value to "re-occupy" the former site of a station that is now inactive to provide some measure of continuity or a reference point from the past. This can be of value even if continuous observations were not made during the entire intervening period.

E.3.2. Element-Specific Factors

E.3.2.1. Temperature: An open exposure with uninhibited air movement is the preferred setting. The most common measurement is made at approximately eye level, 1.5–2.0 m. In snowy locations sensors should be at least one meter higher than the deepest snowpack expected in the next 50 years or perhaps 2–3 times the depth of the average maximum annual depth. Sensors should be shielded above and below from solar radiation (bouncing off snow), from sunrise/sunset horizontal input, and from vertical rock faces. Sensors should be clamped tightly, so that they do not swivel away from level stacks of radiation plates. Nearby vegetation should be kept away from the sensors (several meters). Growing vegetation should be cut to original conditions. Small hollows and swales can cool tremendously at night, and it is best avoid these areas. Side slopes of perhaps a degree or two of angle facilitate air movement and drainage and, in effect, sample a large area during nighttime hours. The very bottom of a valley should be avoided. Temperature can change substantially from moves of only a few meters. Situations have been observed where flat and seemingly uniform conditions (like airport runways) appear to demonstrate different climate behaviors over short distances of a few tens or hundreds of meters (differences of 5–10°C). When snow is on the ground, these microclimatic differences can be stronger, and differences of 2–5°C can occur in the short distance between the thermometer and the snow surface on calm evenings.

E.3.2.2. Precipitation (liquid): Calm locations with vegetative or artificial shielding are preferred. Wind will adversely impact readings; therefore, the less the better. Wind effects on precipitation are far less for rain than for snow. Devices that "save" precipitation present advantages, but most gauges are built to dump precipitation as it falls or to empty periodically. Automated gauges give both the amount and the timing. Simple backups that record only the total precipitation since the last visit have a certain advantage (for example, storage gauges or lengths of PVC pipe perhaps with bladders on the bottom). The following question should be asked: Does the total precipitation from an automated gauge add up to the measured total in a simple bucket (evaporation is prevented with an appropriate substance such as mineral oil)? Drip from overhanging foliage and trees can augment precipitation totals.

E.3.2.3. Precipitation (frozen): Calm locations or shielding are a must. Undercatch for rain is only about 5 percent, but with winds of only 2–4 m/s, gauges may catch only 30–70 percent of the actual snow falling depending on density of the flakes. To catch 100 percent of the snow, the standard configuration for shielding is employed by the CRN (Climate Reference Network): the DFIR (Double-Fence Intercomparison Reference) shield with 2.4-m (8-ft.) vertical, wooden slatted fences in two concentric octagons with diameters of 8 m and 4 m (26 ft and 13 ft, respectively) and an inner Alter shield (flapping vanes). Numerous tests have shown this is the only way to achieve complete catch of snowfall (e.g., Yang et al. 1998, 2001). The DFIR shield is large and bulky; it is recommended that all precipitation gauges have at least Alter shields on them.

Near the coast, much snow is heavy and falls more vertically. In colder locations or storms, light flakes frequently will fly in and then out of the gauge. Clearings in forests are usually excellent sites. Snow blowing from trees that are too close can augment actual precipitation totals. Artificial shielding (vanes, etc.) placed around gauges in snowy locales should always be used if accurate totals are desired. Moving parts tend to freeze up. Capping of gauges during heavy snowfall events is a common occurrence. When the cap becomes pointed, snow falls off to the ground and is not recorded. Caps and plugs often will not fall into the tube until hours, days, or even weeks have passed, typically during an extended period of freezing temperature or above or when sunlight finally occurs. Liquid-based measurements (e.g., SNOTEL "rocket" gauges) do not have the resolution (usually 0.3 cm [0.1 in.] rather than 0.03 cm [0.01 in.]) that tipping bucket and other gauges have but are known to be reasonably accurate in very snowy climates. Light snowfall events might not be recorded until enough of them add up to the next reporting increment. More expensive gauges like Geonors can be considered and could do quite well in snowy settings; however, they need to be emptied every 40 cm (15 in.) or so (capacity of 51 cm [20 in.]) until the new 91-cm (36-in.) capacity gauge is offered for sale. Recently, the NWS has been trying out the new (and very expensive) Ott all-weather gauge. Riming can be an issue in windy foggy environments below freezing. Rime, dew, and other forms of atmospheric condensation are not real precipitation, since they are caused by the gauge.

E.3.2.4. Snow Depth: Windswept areas tend to be blown clear of snow. Conversely, certain types of vegetation can act as a snow fence and cause artificial drifts. However, some amount of vegetation in the vicinity generally can help slow down the wind. The two most common types of snow-depth gauges are the Judd Snow Depth Sensor, produced by Judd Communications, and the snow depth gauge produced by Campbell Scientific, Inc. Opinions vary on which one is better. These gauges use ultrasound and look downward in a cone about 22 degrees in diameter. The ground should be relatively clear of vegetation and maintained in a manner so that the zero point on the calibration scale does not change.

E.3.2.5. Snow Water Equivalent: This is determined by the weight of snow on fluid-filled pads about the size of a desktop set up sometimes in groups of four or in larger hexagons several meters in diameter. These pads require flat ground some distance from nearby sources of windblown snow and shielding that is "just right": not too close to the shielding to act as a kind of snow fence and not too far from the shielding so that blowing and drifting become a factor. Generally, these pads require fluids that possess antifreeze-like properties, as well as handling and replacement protocols.

E.3.2.6. Wind: Open exposures are needed for wind measurements. Small prominences or benches without blockage from certain sectors are preferred. A typical rule for trees is to site stations back 10 tree-heights from all tree obstructions. Sites in long, narrow valleys can obviously only exhibit two main wind directions. Gently rounded eminences are more favored. Any kind of topographic steering should be avoided to the extent possible. Avoiding major mountain chains or single isolated mountains or ridges is usually a favorable approach, if there is a choice. Sustained wind speed and the highest gusts (1-second) should be recorded. Averaging methodologies for both sustained winds and gusts can affect climate trends and should be recorded as metadata with all changes noted. Vegetation growth affects the vertical wind profile, and growth over a few years can lead to changes in mean wind speed even if the "real" wind does not change, so vegetation near the site (perhaps out to 50 m) should be maintained in a quasi-permanent status (same height and spatial distribution). Wind devices can rime up and freeze or spin out of balance. In severely rimed or windy climates, rugged anemometers, such as those made by Taylor, are worth considering. These anemometers are expensive but durable and can withstand substantial abuse. In exposed locations, personnel should plan for winds to be at least 50 m/s and be able to measure these wind speeds. At a minimum, anemometers should be rated to 75 m/s.

E.3.2.7. Humidity: Humidity is a relatively straightforward climate element. Close proximity to lakes or other water features can affect readings. Humidity readings typically are less accurate near 100 percent and at low humidities in cold weather.

E.3.2.8. Solar Radiation: A site with an unobstructed horizon obviously is the most desirable. This generally implies a flat plateau or summit. However, in most locations trees or mountains will obstruct the sun for part of the day.

E.3.2.9. Soil Temperature: It is desirable to measure soil temperature at locations where soil is present. If soil temperature is recorded at only a single depth, the most preferred depth is 10 cm. Other common depths include 25 cm, 50 cm, 2 cm, and 100 cm. Biological activity in the soil will be proportional to temperature with important threshold effects occurring near freezing.

E.3.2.10. Soil Moisture: Soil-moisture gauges are somewhat temperamental and require care to install. The soil should be characterized by a soil expert during installation of the gauge. The readings may require a certain level of experience to interpret correctly. If accurate, readings of soil moisture are especially useful.

E.3.2.11. Distributed Observations: It can be seen readily that compromises must be struck among the considerations described in the preceding paragraphs because some are mutually exclusive.

How large can a "site" be? Generally, the equipment footprint should be kept as small as practical with all components placed next to each other (within less than 10–20 m or so). Readings from one instrument frequently are used to aid in interpreting readings from the remaining instruments.

What is a tolerable degree of separation? Some consideration may be given to locating a precipitation gauge or snow pillow among protective vegetation, while the associated temperature, wind, and humidity readings would be collected more effectively in an open and exposed location within 20–50 m. Ideally, it is advantageous to know the wind measurement precisely at the precipitation gauge, but a compromise involving a short split, and in effect a "distributed observation," could be considered. There are no definitive rules governing this decision, but it is suggested that the site footprint be kept within approximately 50 m. There also are constraints imposed by engineering and electrical factors that affect cable lengths, signal strength, and line noise; therefore, the shorter the cable the better. Practical issues include the need to trench a channel to outlying instruments or to allow lines to lie atop the ground and associated problems with animals, humans, weathering, etc. Separating a precipitation gauge up to 100 m or so from an instrument mast may be an acceptable compromise if other factors are not limiting.

E.3.2.12. Instrument Replacement Schedules: Instruments slowly degrade, and a plan for replacing them with new, refurbished, or recalibrated instruments should be in place. After approximately five years, a systematic change-out procedure should result in replacing most sensors in a network. Certain parts, such as solar radiation sensors, are candidates for annual calibration or change-out. Anemometers tend to degrade as bearings erode or electrical contacts become uneven. Noisy bearings are an indication, and a stethoscope might aid in hearing such noises. Increased internal friction affects the threshold starting speed; once spinning, they tend to function properly. Increases in starting threshold speeds can lead to more zero-wind measurements and thus reduce the reported mean wind speed with no real change in wind properties. A field calibration kit should be developed and taken on all site visits, routine or otherwise. Rain gauges can be tested with drip testers during field visits. Protective conduit and tight water seals can prevent abrasion and moisture problems with the equipment, although seals can keep moisture in as well as out. Bulletproof casings sometimes are employed in remote settings. A supply of spare parts, at least one of each and more for less-expensive or more-delicate sensors, should be maintained to allow replacement of worn or nonfunctional instruments during field visits. In addition, this approach allows instruments to be calibrated in the relative convenience of the operational home—the larger the network, the greater the need for a parts depot.

E.3.3. Long-Term Comparability and Consistency
E.3.3.1. Consistency: The emphasis here is to hold biases constant. Every site has biases, problems, and idiosyncrasies of one sort or another. The best rule to follow is simply to try to keep biases constant through time. Since the goal is to track climate through time, keeping sensors, methodologies, and exposure constant will ensure that only true climate change is being measured. This means leaving the site in its original state or performing maintenance to keep it that way. Once a site is installed, the goal should be to never move the site even by a few meters or to allow significant changes to occur within 100 m for the next several decades.

Sites in or near rock outcroppings likely will experience less vegetative disturbance or growth through the years and will not usually retain moisture, a factor that could speed corrosion. Sites that will remain locally similar for some time are usually preferable. However, in some cases the intent of a station might be to record the local climate effects of changes within a small-scale system (for example, glacier, recently burned area, or scene of some other disturbance) that is subject to a regional climate influence. In this example, the local changes might be much larger than the regional changes.

E.3.3.2. Metadata: Since the climate of every site is affected by features in the immediate vicinity, it is vital to record this information over time and to update the record repeatedly at each service visit. Distances, angles, heights of vegetation, fine-scale topography, condition of instruments, shielding discoloration, and other factors from within a meter to several kilometers should be noted. Systematic photography should be undertaken and updated at least once every one–two years.

Photographic documentation should be taken at each site in a standard manner and repeated every two–three years. Guidelines for methodology were developed by Redmond (2004) as a result of experience with the NOAA CRN and can be found on the WRCC NPS Web pages at http://www.wrcc.dri.edu/nps and at ftp://ftp.wrcc.dri.edu/nps/photodocumentation.pdf.

The main purpose for climate stations is to *track climatic conditions through time*. Anything that affects the interpretation of records through time must to be noted and recorded for posterity. The important factors should be clear to a person who has never visited the site, no matter how long ago the site was installed.

In regions with significant, climatic transition zones, transects are an efficient way to span several climates and make use of available resources. Discussions on this topic at greater detail can be found in Redmond and Simeral (2004) and in Redmond et al. (2005).

E.4. Literature Cited

American Association of State Climatologists. 1985. Heights and exposure standards for sensors on automated weather stations. The State Climatologist **9**.

Brock, F. V., K. C. Crawford, R. L. Elliott, G. W. Cuperus, S. J. Stadler, H. L. Johnson and M. D. Eilts. 1995. The Oklahoma Mesonet: A technical overview. Journal of Atmospheric and Oceanic Technology **12**:5-19.

Daly, C., R. P. Neilson, and D. L. Phillips. 1994. A statistical-topographic model for mapping climatological precipitation over mountainous terrain. Journal of Applied Meteorology **33**:140-158.

Daly, C., W. P. Gibson, G. H. Taylor, G. L. Johnson, and P. Pasteris. 2002. A knowledge-based approach to the statistical mapping of climate. Climate Research **22**:99-113.

Doggett, M., C. Daly, J. Smith, W. Gibson, G. Taylor, G. Johnson, and P. Pasteris. 2004. High-resolution 1971-2000 mean monthly temperature maps for the western United States. Fourteenth AMS Conf. on Applied Climatology, 84th AMS Annual Meeting. Seattle, WA, American Meteorological Society, Boston, MA, January 2004, Paper 4.3, CD-ROM.

Geiger, R., R. H. Aron, and P. E. Todhunter. 2003. The Climate Near the Ground. 6th edition.

Rowman & Littlefield Publishers, Inc., New York.

Gibson, W. P., C. Daly, T. Kittel, D. Nychka, C. Johns, N. Rosenbloom, A. McNab, and G. Taylor. 2002. Development of a 103-year high-resolution climate data set for the conterminous United States. Thirteenth AMS Conf. on Applied Climatology. Portland, OR, American Meteorological Society, Boston, MA, May 2002:181-183.

Goodison, B. E., P. Y. T. Louie, and D. Yang. 1998. WMO solid precipitation measurement intercomparison final report. WMO TD 982, World Meteorological Organization, Geneva, Switzerland.

National Research Council. 1998. Future of the National Weather Service Cooperative Weather Network. National Academies Press, Washington, D.C.

National Research Council. 2001. A Climate Services Vision: First Steps Toward the Future. National Academies Press, Washington, D.C.

Redmond, K. T. 1992. Effects of observation time on interpretation of climatic time series - A need for consistency. Eighth Annual Pacific Climate (PACLIM) Workshop. Pacific Grove, CA, March 1991:141-150.

Redmond, K. T. 2004. Photographic documentation of long-term climate stations. Available from ftp://ftp.wrcc.dri.edu/nps/photodocumentation.pdf. (accessed 15 August 2004)

Redmond, K. T. and D. B. Simeral. 2004. Climate monitoring comments: Central Alaska Network Inventory and Monitoring Program. Available from ftp://ftp.wrcc.dri.edu/nps/alaska/cakn/npscakncomments040406.pdf. (accessed 6 April 2004)

Redmond, K. T., D. B. Simeral, and G. D. McCurdy. 2005. Climate monitoring for southwest Alaska national parks: network design and site selection. Report 05-01. Western Regional Climate Center, Reno, Nevada.

Redmond, K. T., and G. D. McCurdy. 2005. Channel Islands National Park: Design considerations for weather and climate monitoring. Report 05-02. Western Regional Climate Center, Reno, Nevada.

Sevruk, B., and W. R. Hamon. 1984. International comparison of national precipitation gauges with a reference pit gauge. Instruments and Observing Methods, Report No 17, WMO/TD – 38, World Meteorological Organization, Geneva, Switzerland.

Simpson, J. J., Hufford, G. L., C. Daly, J. S. Berg, and M. D. Fleming. 2005. Comparing maps of mean monthly surface temperature and precipitation for Alaska and adjacent areas of Canada produced by two different methods. Arctic **58**:137-161.

Whiteman, C. D. 2000. Mountain Meteorology: Fundamentals and Applications. Oxford University Press, Oxford, UK.

Wilson, E. O. 1998. Consilience: The Unity of Knowledge. Knopf, New York.

World Meteorological Organization. 1983. Guide to meteorological instruments and methods of observation, No. 8, 5th edition, World Meteorological Organization, Geneva Switzerland.

World Meteorological Organization. 2005. Organization and planning of intercomparisons of rainfall intensity gauges. World Meteorological Organization, Geneva Switzerland.

Yang, D., B. E. Goodison, J. R. Metcalfe, V. S. Golubev, R. Bates, T. Pangburn, and C. Hanson. 1998. Accuracy of NWS 8" standard nonrecording precipitation gauge: results and application of WMO intercomparison. Journal of Atmospheric and Oceanic Technology **15**:54-68.

Yang, D., B. E. Goodison, J. R. Metcalfe, P. Louie, E. Elomaa, C. Hanson, V. Bolubev, T. Gunther, J. Milkovic, and M. Lapin. 2001. Compatibility evaluation of national precipitation gauge measurements. Journal of Geophysical Research **106**:1481-1491.

Appendix F. Master metadata field list

Field Name	Field Type	Field Description
begin_date	date	Effective beginning date for a record.
begin_date_flag	char(2)	Flag describing the known accuracy of the begin date for a station.
best_elevation	float(4)	Best known elevation for a station (in feet).
clim_div_code	char(2)	Foreign key defining climate division code (primary in table: clim_div).
clim_div_key	int2	Foreign key defining climate division for a station (primary in table: clim_div.
clim_div_name	varchar(30)	English name for a climate division.
controller_info	varchar(50)	Person or organization who maintains the identifier system for a given weather or climate network.
country_key	int2	Foreign key defining country where a station resides (primary in table: none).
county_key	int2	Foreign key defining county where a station resides (primary in table: county).
county_name	varchar(31)	English name for a county.
Description	text	Any description pertaining to the particular table.
end_date	date	Last effective date for a record.
end_date_flag	char(2)	Flag describing the known accuracy of station end date.
fips_country_code	char(2)	FIPS (federal information processing standards) country code.
fips_state_abbr	char(2)	FIPS state abbreviation for a station.
fips_state_code	char(2)	FIPS state code for a station.
history_flag	char(2)	Describes temporal significance of an individual record among others from the same station.
id_type_key	int2	Foreign key defining the id_type for a station (usually defined in code).
last_updated	date	Date of last update for a record.
Latitude	float(8)	Latitude value.
Longitude	float(8)	Longitude value.
name_type_key	int2	"3": COOP station name, "2": best station name.
Name	varchar(30)	Station name as known at date of last update entry.
ncdc_state_code	char(2)	NCDC, two-character code identifying U.S. state.
network_code	char(8)	Eight-character abbreviation code identifying a network.
network_key	int2	Foreign key defining the network for a station (primary in table: network).
network_station_id	int4	Identifier for a station in the associated network, which is defined by id_type_key.
Remark	varchar(254)	Additional information for a record.
src_quality_code	char(2)	Code describing the data quality for the data source.
state_key	int2	Foreign key defining the U.S. state where a station resides (primary in table: state).
state_name	varchar(30)	English name for a state.
station_alt_name	varchar(30)	Other English names for a station.
station_best_name	varchar(30)	Best, most well-known English name for a station.
time_zone	float4	Time zone where a station resides.
ucan_station_id	int4	Unique station identifier for every station in ACIS.
unit_key	int2	Integer value representing a unit of measure.

93

Field Name	Field Type	Field Description
updated_by	char(8)	Person who last updated a record.
var_major_id	int2	Defines major climate variable.
var_minor_id	int2	Defines data source within a var_major_id.
Zipcode	char(5)	Zipcode where a latitude/longitude point resides.
nps_netcode	char(4)	Network four-character identifier.
nps_netname	varchar(128)	Displayed English name for a network.
Parkcode	char(4)	Park four-character identifier.
Parkname	varchar(128)	Displayed English name for a park/
im_network	char(4)	NPS I&M network where park belongs (a net code)/
station_id	varchar(16)	Station identifier.
station_id_type	varchar(16)	Type of station identifier.
network.subnetwork.id	varchar(16)	Identifier of a sub-network in associated network.
subnetwork_key	int2	Foreign key defining sub-network for a station.
subnetwork_name	varchar(30)	English name for a sub-network.
Slope	integer	Terrain slope at the location.
Aspect	integer	Terrain aspect at the station.
Gps	char(1)	Indicator of latitude/longitude recorded via GPS (global positioning system).
site_description	text(0)	Physical description of site.
route_directions	text(0)	Driving route or site access directions.
station_photo_id	integer	Unique identifier associating a group of photos to a station. Group of photos all taken on same date.
photo_id	char(30)	Unique identifier for a photo.
photo_date	datetime	Date photograph taken.
Photographer	varchar(64)	Name of photographer.
maintenance_date	datetime	Date of station maintenance visit.
contact_key	Integer	Unique identifier associating contact information to a station.
full_name	varchar(64)	Full name of contact person.
Organization	varchar(64)	Organization of contact person.
contact_type	varchar(32)	Type of contact person (operator, administrator, etc.)
position_title	varchar(32)	Title of contact person.
Address	varchar(32)	Address for contact person.
City	varchar(32)	City for contact person.
State	varchar(2)	State for contact person.
zip_code	char(10)	Zipcode for contact person.
Country	varchar(32)	Country for contact person.
Email	varchar(64)	E-mail for contact person.
work_phone	varchar(16)	Work phone for contact person.
contact_notes	text(254)	Other details regarding contact person.
equipment_type	char(30)	Sensor measurement type; i.e., wind speed, air temperature, etc.
eq_manufacturer	char(30)	Manufacturer of equipment.
eq_model	char(20)	Model number of equipment.
serial_num	char(20)	Serial number of equipment.
eq_description	varchar(254)	Description of equipment.
install_date	datetime	Installation date of equipment.
remove_date	datetime	Removal date of equipment.
ref_height	integer	Sensor displacement height from surface.
sampling_interval	varchar(10)	Frequency of sensor measurement.

Appendix G. Electronic supplements

G.1. ACIS metadata file for weather and climate stations associated with the NETN:
http://www.wrcc.dri.edu/nps/pub/NETN/metadata/NETN_from_ACIS.tar.gz.

G.2. NETN metadata files for weather and climate stations associated with the NETN:
http://www.wrcc.dri.edu/nps/pub/NETN/metadata/NETN_NPS.tar.gz.

Appendix H. Descriptions of weather/climate-monitoring networks

H.1. Clean Air Status and Trends Network (CASTNet)
- Purpose of network: provide information for evaluating the effectiveness of national emission-control strategies.
- Primary management agency: EPA.
- Data website: http://epa.gov/castnet/.
- Measured weather/climate elements:
  - Air temperature.
  - Precipitation.
  - Relative humidity.
  - Wind speed.
  - Wind direction.
  - Wind gust.
  - Gust direction.
  - Solar radiation.
  - Soil moisture and temperature.
- Sampling frequency: hourly.
- Reporting frequency: hourly.
- Estimated station cost: $13000.
- Network strengths:
  - High-quality data.
  - Sites are well maintained.
- Network weaknesses:
  - Density of station coverage is low.
  - Shorter periods of record for western United States.

CASTNet primarily is an air-quality-monitoring network managed by the EPA. The elements shown here are intended to support interpretation of measured air-quality parameters such as ozone, nitrates, sulfides, etc., which also are measured at CASTNet sites.

H.2. NWS Cooperative Observer Program (COOP)
- Purpose of network:
  - Provide observational, meteorological data required to define U.S. climate and help measure long-term climate changes.
  - Provide observational, meteorological data in near real-time to support forecasting and warning mechanisms and other public service programs of the NWS.
- Primary management agency: NOAA (NWS).
- Data website: data are available from the NCDC (http://www.ncdc.noaa.gov), RCCs (e.g., WRCC, http://www.wrcc.dri.edu), and state climate offices.
- Measured weather/climate elements
  - Maximum, minimum, and observation-time temperature.
  - Precipitation, snowfall, snow depth.
  - Pan evaporation (some stations).

- Sampling frequency: daily.
- Reporting frequency: daily or monthly (station-dependent).
- Estimated station cost: $2000 with maintenance costs of $500–900/year.
- Network strengths:
  o Decade–century records at most sites.
  o Widespread national coverage (thousands of stations).
  o Excellent data quality when well maintained.
  o Relatively inexpensive; highly cost effective.
  o Manual measurements; not automated.
- Network weaknesses:
  o Uneven exposures; many are not well-maintained.
  o Dependence on schedules for volunteer observers.
  o Slow entry of data from many stations into national archives.
  o Data subject to observational methodology; not always documented.
  o Manual measurements; not automated and not hourly.

The COOP network has long served as the main climate observation network in the United States. Readings are usually made by volunteers using equipment supplied, installed, and maintained by the federal government. The observer in effect acts as a host for the data-gathering activities and supplies the labor; this is truly a "cooperative" effort. The SAO sites often are considered to be part of the cooperative network as well if they collect the previously mentioned types of weather/climate observations. Typical observation days are morning to morning, evening to evening, or midnight to midnight. By convention, observations are ascribed to the date the instrument was reset at the end of the observational period. For this reason, midnight observations represent the end of a day. The Historical Climate Network is a subset of the cooperative network but contains longer and more complete records.

H.3. Citizen Weather Observer Program (CWOP)
- Purpose of network: collect observations from private citizens and make these data available for homeland security and other weather applications, providing constant feedback to the observers to maintain high data quality.
- Primary management agency: NOAA MADIS program.
- Data Website: http://www.wxqa.com.
- Measured weather/climate elements:
  o Air temperature.
  o Dewpoint temperature.
  o Precipitation.
  o Wind speed and direction.
  o Barometric pressure.
- Sampling frequency: 15 minutes or less.
- Reporting frequency: 15 minutes.
- Estimated station cost: unknown.
- Network strengths:
  o Active partnership between public agencies and private citizens.
  o Large number of participant sites.

o Regular communications between data providers and users, encouraging higher data quality.
- Network weaknesses:
   o Variable instrumentation platforms.
   o Metadata are sometimes limited.

The CWOP network is a public-private partnership with U.S. citizens and various agencies including NOAA, NASA (National Aeronautics and Space Administration), and various universities. There are over 4500 registered sites worldwide, with close to 3000 of these sites located in North America.

H.4. NPS Gaseous Pollutant Monitoring Program (GPMP)
- Purpose of network: measurement of ozone and related meteorological elements.
- Primary management agency: NPS.
- Data website: http://www2.nature.nps.gov/air/monitoring.
- Measured weather/climate elements:
   o Air temperature.
   o Relative humidity.
   o Precipitation.
   o Wind speed and direction.
   o Solar radiation.
   o Surface wetness.
- Sampling frequency: continuous.
- Reporting frequency: hourly.
- Estimated station cost: unknown.
- Network strengths:
   o Stations are located within NPS park units.
   o Data quality is excellent, with high data standards.
   o Provides unique measurements that are not available elsewhere.
   o Records are up to 2 decades in length.
   o Site maintenance is excellent.
   o Thermometers are aspirated.
- Network weaknesses:
   o Not easy to download the entire data set or to ingest live data.
   o Period of record is short compared to other automated networks. Earliest sites date from 2004.
   o Station spacing and coverage: station installation is episodic, driven by opportunistic situations.

The NPS web site indicates that there are 33 sites with continuous ozone analysis run by NPS, with records from a few to about 16-17 years. Of these stations, 12 are labeled as GPMP sites and the rest are labeled as CASTNet sites. All of these have standard meteorological measurements, including a 10-m mast. Another nine GPMP sites are located within NPS units but run by cooperating agencies. A number of other sites (1-2 dozen) ran for differing periods in the past, generally less than 5-10 years.

H.5. NOAA Ground-Based GPS Meteorology (GPS-MET)

- Purpose of network:
  - Measure atmospheric water vapor using ground-based GPS receivers.
  - Facilitate use of these data operational and in other research and applications.
  - Provides data for weather forecasting, atmospheric modeling and prediction, climate monitoring, calibrating and validation other observing systems including radiosondes and satellites, and research.
- Primary management agency: NOAA Earth System Research Laboratory.
- Data website: http://gpsmet.noaa.gov/jsp/index.jsp.
- Measurements:
  - Dual frequency carrier phase measurements every 30 seconds
- Ancillary weather/climate observations:
  - Air temperature.
  - Relative humidity.
  - Pressure.
- Reporting frequency: currently 30 min.
- Estimated station cost: $0-$10K, depending on approach. Data from dual frequency GPS receivers installed for conventional applications (e.g. high accuracy surveying) can be used without modification.
- Network strengths:
  - Frequent, high-quality measurements.
  - High reliability.
  - All-weather operability.
  - Many uses.
  - Highly leveraged.
  - Requires no calibration.
  - Measurement accuracy improves with time.
- Network weakness:
  - Point measurement.
  - Provides no direct information about the vertical distribution of water vapor.

The GPS-MET network is the first network of its kind dedicated to GPS meteorology (see Duan et al. 1996). The GPS-MET network was developed in response to the need for improved moisture observations to support weather forecasting, climate monitoring, and other research activities. GPS-MET is a collaboration between NOAA and several other governmental and university organizations and institutions.

GPS meteorology utilizes the radio signals broadcast by the satellite Global Positioning System for atmospheric remote sensing. GPS meteorology applications have evolved along two paths: ground-based (Bevis et al. 1992) and space-based (Yuan et al. 1993). Both applications make the same fundamental measurement (the apparent delay in the arrival of radio signals caused by changes in the radio-refractivity of the atmosphere along the paths of the radio signals) but they do so from different perspectives.

In ground-based GPS meteorology, a GPS receiver and antenna are placed at a fixed location on the ground and the signals from all GPS satellites in view are continuously recorded. From this information, the exact position of the GPS antenna can be determined over time with high (millimeter-level) accuracy. Subsequent measurements of the antenna position are compared with the known position, and the differences can be attributed to changes in the temperature, pressure and water vapor in the atmosphere above the antenna. By making continuous measurements of temperature and pressure at the site, the total amount of water vapor in the atmosphere at this location can be estimated with high accuracy under all weather conditions. For more information on ground based GPS meteorology the reader is referred to http://gpsmet.noaa.gov.

In space-based GPS meteorology, GPS receivers and antennas are placed on satellites in Low Earth Orbit (LEO), and the signals transmitted by a GPS satellite are continuously recorded as a GPS satellite "rises" or "sets" behind the limb of the Earth. This process is called an occultation or a limb sounding. The GPS radio signals bend more as they encounter a thicker atmosphere and the bending (which causes an apparent increase in the length of the path of the radio signal) can be attributed to changes in temperature, pressure and water vapor along the path of the radio signal through the atmosphere that is nominally about 300 km long. The location of an occultation depends on the relative geometries of the GPS satellites in Mid Earth Orbit and the satellites in LEO. As a consequence, information about the vertical temperature, pressure and moisture structure of the Earth's atmosphere as a whole can be estimated with high accuracy, but not at any one particular place over time. The main difference between ground and space-based GPS meteorology is one of geometry. A space-based measurement can be thought of as a ground-based measurement turned on its side. For more information on space based GPS meteorology, the reader is referred to http://www.cosmic.ucar.edu/gpsmet/.

H.6. Remote Automated Weather Station Network (RAWS)

- Purpose of network: provide near-real-time (hourly or near hourly) measurements of meteorological variables for use in fire weather forecasts and climatology. Data from RAWS also are used for natural resource management, flood forecasting, natural hazard management, and air-quality monitoring.
- Primary management agency: WRCC, National Interagency Fire Center.
- Data website: http://www.raws.dri.edu/index.html.
- Measured weather/climate elements:
  o Air temperature.
  o Precipitation.
  o Relative humidity.
  o Wind speed.
  o Wind direction.
  o Wind gust.
  o Gust direction.
  o Solar radiation.
  o Soil moisture and temperature.
- Sampling frequency: 1 or 10 minutes, element-dependent.
- Reporting frequency: generally hourly. Some stations report every 15 or 30 minutes.
- Estimated station cost: $12000 with satellite telemetry ($8000 without satellite telemetry); maintenance costs are around $2000/year.
- Network strengths:

- o Metadata records are usually complete.
- o Sites are located in remote areas.
- o Sites are generally well-maintained.
- o Entire period of record available on-line.
- Network weaknesses:
  - o RAWS network is focused largely on fire management needs (formerly focused only on fire needs).
  - o Frozen precipitation is not measured reliably.
  - o Station operation is not always continuous.
  - o Data transmission is completed via one-way telemetry. Data are therefore recoverable either in real-time or not at all.

The RAWS network is used by many land-management agencies, such as the BLM, NPS, Fish and Wildlife Service, Bureau of Indian Affairs, Forest Service, and other agencies. The RAWS network was one of the first automated weather station networks to be installed in the United States. Most gauges do not have heaters, so hydrologic measurements are of little value when temperatures dip below freezing or reach freezing after frozen precipitation events. There are approximately 1100 real-time sites in this network and about 1800 historic sites (some are decommissioned or moved). The sites can transmit data all winter but may be in deep snow in some locations. The WRCC is the archive for this network and receives station data and metadata through a special connection to the National Interagency Fire Center in Boise, Idaho.

H.7. NWS/FAA Surface Airways Observation Network (SAO)
- Purpose of network: provide near-real-time (hourly or near hourly) measurements of meteorological variables and are used both for airport operations and weather forecasting.
- Primary management agency: NOAA, FAA.
- Data website: data are available from state climate offices, RCCs (e.g., WRCC, http://www.wrcc.dri.edu), and NCDC (http://www.ncdc.noaa.gov).
- Measured weather/climate elements:
  - o Air temperature.
  - o Dewpoint and/or relative humidity.
  - o Wind speed.
  - o Wind direction.
  - o Wind gust.
  - o Gust direction.
  - o Barometric pressure.
  - o Precipitation (not at many FAA sites).
  - o Sky cover.
  - o Ceiling (cloud height).
  - o Visibility.
- Sampling frequency: element-dependent.
- Reporting frequency: element-dependent.
- Estimated station cost: $100000–$200000, with maintenance costs approximately $10000/year.
- Network strengths:
  - o Records generally extend over several decades.

- o Consistent maintenance and station operations.
- o Data record is reasonably complete and usually high quality.
- o Hourly or sub-hourly data.
- Network weaknesses:
  - o Nearly all sites are located at airports.
  - o Data quality can be related to size of airport—smaller airports tend to have poorer datasets.
  - o Influences from urbanization and other land-use changes.

These stations are managed by NOAA, U. S. Navy, U. S. Air Force, and FAA. These stations are located generally at major airports and military bases. The FAA stations often do not record precipitation, or they may provide precipitation records of reduced quality. Automated stations are typically ASOSs for the NWS or AWOSs for the FAA. Some sites only report episodically with observers paid per observation.

H.8. Weather For You Network (WX4U)
- Purpose of network: allow volunteer weather enthusiasts around the U.S. to observe and share weather data.
- Data website: http://www.met.utah.edu/jhorel/html/mesonet.
- Measured weather/climate elements:
  - o Air temperature.
  - o Relative humidity and dewpoint temperature.
  - o Precipitation.
  - o Wind speed and direction.
  - o Wind gust and direction.
  - o Pressure.
- Sampling frequency: 10 minutes.
- Reporting frequency: 10 minutes.
- Estimated station cost: unknown.
- Network strengths:
  - o Stations are located throughout the U.S.
  - o Stations provide near-real-time observations.
- Network weaknesses:
  - o Instrumentation platforms can be variable.
  - o Data are sometimes of questionable quality.

The WX4U network is a nationwide collection of weather stations run by local observers. Meteorological elements that are measured usually include temperature, precipitation, wind, and humidity.

NPS/NETN/NRTR—2006/011, November 2006